successful scholarship

successful scholarship

Walter Pauk
Cornell University

Prentice-Hall, Inc., Englewood Cliffs, New Jersey

PRENTICE-HALL INTERNATIONAL, INC., *London*
PRENTICE-HALL OF AUSTRALIA, PTY. LTD., *Sydney*
PRENTICE-HALL OF CANADA, LTD., *Toronto*
PRENTICE-HALL OF INDIA (PRIVATE) LTD., *New Delhi*
PRENTICE-HALL OF JAPAN, INC., *Tokyo*

preface

Each article in this book has a contribution to make to the most important aspect of college life: the academic side. To be sure, there are other important aspects of college life (fraternities, sororities, athletics, etc.), but these activities are meaningful only if they revolve around successful scholarship. When academic failure replaces successful scholarship, the picture changes: the light extracurricular activities which brought fullness to the college campus now become distracting frivolities which may have, in fact, contributed to academic failure. To maintain a proper balance, successful scholarship, then, must remain the focal point of college life.

I have assembled these articles to help students understand better the process of scholarship, not through platitudinous "advice"; rather through the wisdom of men who have lived active intellectual lives. For example, who could write as insightfully and beautifully on "Habit" as William James; or on the classical education as courageously and clearly as Robert Hutchins?

You, the student, will find practical advice in the prefatory comments preceding each of the main parts and each of the articles. This advice—these comments—are based on years of experience gained through teaching courses in reading and study skills to thousands of college students, as well as counsel given to hundreds of students who had come to the Cornell Reading-Study Center for help.

I realize that in some cases my comments have gone beyond the bounds of advice. They have actually become exhortations so that the ideas and techniques indispensable to good scholarship would not be missed.

You will notice, too, that there are ten questions at the end of each article. I included these questions for two reasons: First, to help you gain a more thorough understanding of each article—more thorough than a single cursory reading would yield; and second, to provide you with a means of realistic practice in developing ten specific reading skills which are necessary if you are to comprehend literature adequately at the college level.

Remember that each question is designed to teach you a skill which is both necessary and basic. If you master these skills so that they become almost second nature, then you will come closer to the traditional concept of a "reader" than most students you may know. These ten skills will enable you not just to read, or to read more quickly, but to read with precision and awareness, with a sensitivity based on perception and discrimination.

Before I close a word should be said in thanks to the many people whose encouragement and material aid have made this book possible. Appreciation is expressed to the authors and publishers for their permission to reprint the articles of which they hold copyright. My students, especially in seminars, have taught me much, and many of them have graciously given permission to use some of their ideas and suggestions. I am grateful to all of them.

Special thanks is due to Mr. Charles Dwyer, Mr. Robert Wuerthner, and Mr. Michael D'Elia, all of Cornell University, and Mr. Alan Krech, instructor at Corning Community College, Corning, New York for field testing many of the ideas and techniques included in this book.

Finally, I am eternally grateful to Mrs. Laura Relyea for her competent and always willing assistance in carrying the major burden in the preparation of the manuscript.

WALTER PAUK

Ithaca, New York

contents

introduction

Most people would like to improve their reading skills, but don't know how to go about doing so. Some try by reading about reading, others by using mechanical gadgets, while still others by taking courses in speed reading. None of these approaches has really led to better reading, primarily because of two serious omissions: First, a person's weaknesses in reading skills are not identified; and second, even if weaknesses were identified, no provision is made for overcoming them.

It is usually agreed that reading is a general ability made up of specific skills, such as perceiving the author's main ideas, his intention, his tone, and so forth. It would seem necessary, therefore, that in any program designed to improve reading, these three criteria should be met: first, a means for identifying strengths, and particularly weaknesses in reading; second, instruction on how to correct weaknesses; and third, material on which to practice the suggestions made for correcting weaknesses.

To provide for the first step, this book contains (on page xii) a diagnostic instrument, the Cornell Diagnostic Chart, to identify your strengths and weaknesses in dealing with ten important comprehension skills; second, the Appendix contains instructional material on each of these ten skills; and third, twenty carefully selected articles, with questions, provide materials on which to practice applying and refining these skills so necessary to intelligent reading.

The chart is a diagnostic instrument because of its special construction. The design is as follows: as mentioned previously, each article in this book is followed by ten questions. The first important innovation is that each question is designed to tap one of the following comprehension skills: meaning of words in context, understanding statements explicitly made, interpreting allusions and figures of speech, recognizing patterns of development, recognizing the use of emotive words, recognizing the author's tone, grasping the moral or philosophical attitude, making correct inferences, recognizing the functions of descriptive elements, and determining the author's intent.

The second innovation is that the questions are always in the same position for every selection; that is, the question designed to test your skill to ascertain the meanings of words in context is always Question 1, the question designed to test your skill to understand statements explicitly made is always Question 2, and so on.

Third, since all of your answers to all of these selections must be placed on the Diagnostic Chart, you will see at a glance the questions which you regularly answer correctly, and more important, the ones which you answer incorrectly. For instance, after completing but three articles, a definite pattern might emerge; that is, if you find that for the first three selections you have gotten three X's (symbol for incorrect) in the column for Question 4, then you can safely assume that you need help specifically in finding out how "to recognize the author's plan" for developing his article.

Whenever a weakness in comprehension, Question 4 for example, is indicated by the Diagnostic Chart, you can help yourself to overcome it by following this procedure: First, turn to the instructional material pertaining to Question 4 which is found in the Appendix; second, study the material until you believe that you have a better understanding of how to ascertain "the author's plan for developing his article"; third, go back to the article last read, number three for example; fourth, re-read Question 4 carefully, fixing in mind the correct answer; fifth, reread the entire article with the single purpose of looking for the organizational pattern; sixth, after a careful reading, turn to the question again to see why the other three choices do not fit the article's actual organizational pattern as well as why the correct answer does fit the case; seventh, follow the same procedure for articles one and two.

After analyzing and studying to overcome your weakness, the chances are good that you will succeed in answering correctly Question 4 when you encounter it in the next new article. Perchance you still fail in answering Question 4 correctly on the next article, arranging a conference with your instructor would be a wise step.

Many scholars believe that real learning is best acquired when you have to figure out the answers by yourself. One famous scholar, John Henry Newman, says:

> Self-education in any shape, in the most restricted sense, is preferable to a system of teaching which, professing so much, really does so little for the mind.

This self-diagnosing chart, I firmly believe, sets up an ideal situation where so very much can be done for genuinely developing the mind through self-education.

to the student

The answer key has been placed on the page facing the Diagnostic Chart (after the cover sheet is removed) to facilitate your checking answers quickly and accurately, and to preclude the vexing and frustrating chore of flipping pages back and forth. To gain the maximum amount of practice and learning from answering the questions at the end of each article, the following procedures and techniques are recommended:

1. *Use the "dot" technique.* This is not a required step, but if used will help you make genuine progress in reading ability. This is how it works: After reading an article but once, make a nonofficial attempt to answer all ten questions by placing a light dot alongside the choice which you believe is correct. Go through all ten questions in this manner. Remember that real learning takes place best when extra effort is expended.

After completing this preliminary step, you may now reread carefully the article as many times as you like to answer the questions officially; that is, this time draw a circle around the letter (*a, b, c,* or *d*) to indicate your final choice.

After having used this technique, most students reported experiencing intellectual pleasure as they either confirmed the nonofficial answer after having reread the article, or found where and why they had erred. In addition, some students reported great improvement in concentration, perception, and retention.

2. After having made your official choice of *a, b, c,* or *d* by encircling, transfer these answers to the Cornell Diagnostic Chart. You have now placed your answers in proper categories.

3. The next step is to compare your answers with those in the answer key. Do not clutter up the Chart with "*x's*" and "*c's*"; rather, write the correct letter above the incorrect one, and leave the correct answers unmarked; thus, to tally your score, all you need do is count the spaces with two letters in them. Assign ten points to each incorrect answer, subtract the total from one hundred, and the difference is your score.

4. After having completed three articles, look over your Chart to spot any patterns which have developed or seem to be developing. If a weakness is spotted, then follow the instructions given in the Preface on how to use the instructional materials in the Appendix.

CORNELL DIAGNOSTIC CHART
(↓ = Record Answers Vertically)

	1	2	3	4	5	6	7	8	9	10	11	12	13	14	15	16	17	18	19	20
I																				
II																				
III																				
IV																				
V																				
VI																				
VII																				
VIII																				
IX																				
X																				

keep
this sheet over the answer key
on page xv
until you have completed transferring
all of the answers
to the proper spaces on the Diagnostic Chart.

then
tear along perforations and remove.

ANSWER KEY

	1	2	3	4	5	6	7	8	9	10	11	12	13	14	15	16	17	18	19	20
I	B	C	C	C	B	C	B	A	B	B	A	D	A	D	C	D	B	C	C	D
II	C	B	D	C	C	C	B	C	D	C	A	C	A	B	A	D	D	D	C	D
III	A	D	D	D	A	A	C	D	D	D	A	C	A	D	A	D	D	A	D	
IV	C	B	A	A	D	A	D	C	D	D	A	D	D	D	A	A	C	A	C	D
V	D	A	D	D	A	C	D	D	C	B	B	D	B	A	D	B	C	B	D	B
VI	A	B	B	B	A	A	A	B	A	A	B	D	C	A	A	A	A	B	B	B
VII	B	B	D	B	B	D	D	C	D	C	A	C	D	B	B	C	C	A	A	D
VIII	D	C	B	C	B	A	A	C	D	C	A	D	B	C	C	B	A	C	B	C
IX	C	A	C	D	D	D	D	D	C	C	C	D	C	D	A	D	D	A	D	D
X	A	D	C	C	A	C	D	B	C	C	A	A	A	B	A	A	A	A	B	B

TYPES OF QUESTIONS: DESCRIPTIVE CAPTIONS

I. Words in Context
II. Explicit Statements
III. Allusions and Figures of Speech
IV. Patterns of Development
V. Emotive Words

VI. Author's Tone
VII. Moral or Philosophical Attitude
VIII. Author's Implications
IX. Descriptive Elements
X. Author's Intent

part i

On Becoming Fully Educated

Each person must make up his own mind about the worth of college and what he wants to get out of college. You have, no doubt, already received much advice and will continue to receive much more throughout all of your college days. You will surely hear conflicting views, and perhaps will find it difficult to judge which view, if any, is close to the truth.

There is no sure way, but I would rather take my chances at getting close to the truth by first reading some of the best thinkers and educators of our day.

One distinct advantage in reading the next two selections is that you may read, re-read, ponder, and discuss these writings. When you have done so, you will have grown to some extent—some of the ideas read and pondered will become a part of you—consequently, you will not enter the market place of discussion empty handed; rather you will enter with a standard which can be held, modified, or departed from.

By reading and thinking now, you will not be buffeted into confusion; for now, you will have a point of view.

1

comments

Why Go to College

Though I have skipped or skimmed many of the longer articles which I have encountered while reading for pleasure, I have never done this with any article, regardless of length, written by Robert Maynard Hutchins.

Robert Hutchins became Dean of the Yale Law School at an early age and president of the University of Chicago when only thirty.

He is generally known for his unconventional theories about higher education, and specifically for his belief that a university education should revolve around the reading of the classics.

Many readers also admire Hutchins' style of writing which is direct, honest, and vigorous.

Why Go to College?

Robert M. Hutchins

Most American parents want to send their children to college. And their children, for the most part, are anxious to go. It is an American tradition that there is something about a college that transforms an ordinary infant

Robert M. Hutchins, "Why Go To College? *The Saturday Evening Post* (January 22, 1938). Reprinted by permission of the author.

into a superior adult. Men and women who have been to college some-times suspect that this is not the case, but they seldom say so. They are alumni, and, as such, it is their life work to maintain the tradition that college—their college anyway—is the greatest place in the world.

College is the greatest place in the world for those who ought to go to college and who go for the right reasons. For those who ought not to go to college or who go for the wrong reasons, college is a waste of time and money.

Who should go to college? In order to answer this question, we might well begin by deciding who should not. My experience with college, as student, teacher, and commencement orator, convinces me that the following persons should not go to college:

Children whose parents have no other reason for sending them than that they can afford to.

Children whose parents have no other reason for sending them than to get them off their hands for four years.

Children whose characters are bad and whose parents believe that college will change them for the better.

Children who have no other reason for going to college than to avoid work or have a good time for four years.

Children who have no other reason for going to college than to have a stadium in which to demonstrate their athletic ability.

Children who have no other reason for going to college than the notion that it will help them achieve social or financial success in later life.

These children should be kept at home, or they should be sent to a country club, a trade school, or a body-building institute. There is, or should be, no place for them in an institution whose only excuse for existing is the training of the mind.

If we may then proceed to the original question—"Who should go to college?"—I submit the following answer:

Anyone should go to college who has demonstrated both an aptitude and a desire for more education than he has been able to get in elementary and high school. And I may add that to deprive any such person of a college education because his parents cannot afford to give him one is to commit an offense not only against the individual but also against society at large.

One of the surprising aspects of American society is its indifference to poor men's sons and daughters who give promise of leadership in the national life. It is true that we have scholarships and devices for self-support of college students. But our scholarships are too few to begin to accommodate those who deserve them. And self-support means that a college student who needs all his time to get an education has to devote half of it to earning a living.

There is something of true nobility about the boy—or girl—who works his way through school. To such young people as these, education is an opportunity, not a ritual. It means the sacrifice of gaiety at the age when gaiety is prized highest. It means work, work, and more work. The individual who survives this grueling experience is likely to display a high order of industry and courage his life long. But it is precisely because the self-supporting student is likely to be the worthiest student that he should be relieved of the burden of self-support. If, instead of holding down a job from four to eight hours a day, he is able to devote those hours to the development of his mind, our country might produce more Michelsons, Holmeses and Deweys.

In England, a country which has produced more than its share of the world's leaders, the number of scholarships is such that almost no boy or girl who deserves a college education goes without one. It is said that half the students at Oxford and Cambridge are there on scholarships. The Scotch have the world's most comprehensive system for discovering promising young people and supporting them in college. Hence the Scotch rule England.

Those who should go to college should go to get an education. Because the colleges of the United States have allowed themselves to be used for purposes other than education, it has never been easier than it is today, for those who can afford it, to get into college. Nor has it ever been easier to stay in college and be graduated. The only thing that is really difficult to do is get an education. If, however, a young person came to me and told me he wanted to get an education, I would preach him a sermon somewhat as follows:

You can get an education in college if you try. But you must bring three things with you: A certain minimum intellectual equipment, habits of work, and an interest in getting an education. Without them, you can still get into college and stay there for four years. You can have a good time; you can keep out of trouble; you can get a degree and become a full-fledged alumnus with a proprietary interest in all subsequent football scores; but you cannot get an education.

With them, you can get an education and become an enlightened human being. Every college library contains the world's great books. They will not be out when you ask for them. And there is scarcely a college in America that does not have on its faculty at least a few men who have refused to let themselves be used for purposes other than education. It will not be difficult to find them. They will familiarize you with the leading ideas in their own fields. They will interest you in the relations between their own and other fields. And they will suggest how, when you have fulfilled the comparatively easy requirements of your courses, you can educate yourself.

Unless you find these men and listen to them, unless you find the books you should read and read them, you will find college, aside from social life and athletics, a dull place. You will find that college, like the rest of the educational system, is set up for what is known as the "average" student. When you apply for admission, no one will ask you, "What do you know?" You will be asked instead, "How many years have you spent in school?" Your high school credits will be examined, and if you have succeeded in obtaining "average" grades by bringing the teacher an apple, or by memorizing the dates of Shakespeare's birth and death, you will be admitted to the Elysian fields of higher learning. The occasional college which has some additional criteria for admission does not demand much more. Then, you will find that in college, as in high school, you have only to study the professors and memorize some more information.

You will be filled with countless useless facts, sixty per cent of which you will have to repeat to pass countless tests. You may find your intellectual interest stifled by the hopeless prospect of acquiring all the miscellaneous information you are told you must possess. You will tread your weary round, picking up a fragment here and a fragment there, until you have been examined on fragment after fragment and served your time.

This is the fate that awaits you unless you are determined to hew your way through the underbrush of mediocrity and get an education. When you come to college determined to get one, you will find yourself confused at the beginning. Your previous schooling has done little more than teach you, in a broad way, how to read and write; it takes a person ten or twelve years to learn how to do those two things well. When you come to college, you will be interested in acquiring an understanding of the leading ideas in each great field of knowledge. It will require hard work on your part to master these ideas, but students before you have mastered them and few of them were geniuses. So you will not let the appearance of confusion confuse you; you will buckle down to the business at hand and avoid, in so far as it is possible, the pleasant distractions of the campus.

At the end of your first semester or your first year, you will return home to visit your parents. They will want to know what you have learned, and you will try to tell them. Even if you have been determined to get an education, you will be only partly educated, so what you tell them may disturb them. Being only partly educated, you may be most excited by the ideas which, when you have become fully educated, you will realize were among the least important you encountered. If your parents are wise, they will wait until you are fully educated before they decide whether your education has been worth the expense.

Wise as your parents may be, they may have been influenced by the traditional American attitude toward college. They may want to know whether you made the freshman team, the college paper, or a "good" fraternity. Perhaps you have had the agility to get on the team, the time to try out for the paper, or the money and clothes to get into a "good" fraternity. Perhaps you have had none of these prerequisites for extracurricular achievement. Perhaps you have had some or all of the prerequisites, but have discovered that getting an education requires all your agility and all your time. In any case, you will inform your misguided parents that much as you hate to disappoint them, you came to college to get an education and cannot be held accountable for failing to get anything else.

You will return to college at the end of your first semester or your first year and pursue your studies. They will get harder as you go along. You will have to think harder and work harder. And the college which you are attending may make it hard to stick to the business of getting an education. For the college you are attending will probably be one that is distinguished for its financial resources, its athletic facilities, and its social advantages; most American colleges are. You will have comfortable quarters and good food. Gentlemen purchased at what, for the teaching profession, are good salaries will exert themselves to keep you amused. Gentlemen purchased at even higher salaries will exert themselves to keep you employed in the gymnasium and on the athletic field. Your associates will be gentlemen. You will like them and they will like you. If you expend no more effort on your courses than you have to, you will find little difficulty in passing them, for they are adjusted to the ability of the average student. This is the unrippled stream of "college life" down which you may meander if you want to.

Do you want to? My classmates and I did. We went to college to go through the formalities, to become college men, to get to know the fellows. The fellows we got to know were those who provided us with the gayest amusements and the most profitable relationships and who afterward formed a great brotherhood ready and willing to help out, socially, politically, and financially, those of the brethren who were down on their luck.

The stock of prejudices we brought with us to college remained largely unimpaired when we left it. If we had our corners knocked off, and thus got a kind of education, it was largely because we were associated with a lot of bright young men who took peculiar pleasure in jumping on people for the slightest deviation from the normal. We didn't care to be jumped on, so we never deviated from the normal after we found out what it was.

It was not normal then to depart from the traditional apparel. We all wore the same kind of clothes, just as you are expected to, the only difference being that our coat and pants had to match and yours must not. It was not normal to be sentimental about the college, except in song, nor was it normal to be friendly in conversation unless our remarks were prefaced by enough insults to show that we were manly.

We gradually grew into the likeness of one another, and a rather pleasant likeness we thought it was too. We had the conviction that the society of the great world would welcome us. And so it did, on the whole. The ideals of our era were conformity and "getting ahead." We had already achieved conformity, and we looked as if we would "get ahead," so the world welcomed us.

It made the mistake of believing we were educated. It did not take the trouble, nor did it know how, to discover that we were not. How could we be? College life had offered us a great many things, including education. We had imbibed deeply of those features that were pleasantest and most admired by the outside world. We had not insisted on getting an education, and college had not insisted that we either get one or get out and make room for people who wanted one.

Now that we are old and kicking around in a world which is worse off than it was before we entered it, we wonder if we might not have acquired the social and physical graces by spending four years in the YMCA or the Elks. These bodies have high ideals, they are organized for mutual improvement and good fellowship, and their dues are lower than the tuition our parents laid out for our college education.

If you ignore your opportunity as we ignored ours, the world may not let you off as easily as it did us. If you go to college, you will do well to insist on getting an education, as we did not.

As I look around me from the vantage point of my advanced years, I am unconvinced, unlike many of my colleagues, that it is any easier to get a real education today than it was in the Gay 20's. The depression no more sobered the colleges and the universities than it sobered the nation at large. With the return of material prosperity to certain areas of the population, our institutions of higher learning are as much concerned with the social and physical welfare of their students as they were before the crash. This concern may please parents whose ideals remain the ideals of the 20's, but it interferes with giving and getting an education.

Fraternity houses and stadiums are again filled. College and university presidents are setting the pace for the students by promoting programs of expansion and beautification which have little to do with education. Education and scholarship can be carried on in ramshackle buildings. As a university president, I should not expect a university to refuse gifts of beautiful and useful buildings. As a sociable human being, I should not expect a college or university to ignore the social side of life. I should insist, however, that colleges and universities place first things first. The emphasis on the nonintellectual aspects of college life can only stimulate students everywhere to emphasize fraternities, good manners, and athletics. This emphasis the country does not need.

As one who has been a "fraternity man" in his day, I think I appreciate the advantages and the evils of this ancient form of comradeship. On the credit side, it may be said that no fraternity ever made a bum of a man. The man who leaves college a bum brought his taste for being a bum to college with him. His character or lack of it, was already crystallized when he arrived at the age of eighteen. If he had the impulse to "bull" all day and play poker all night, he devoted himself to these arts whether his base of operation was a fraternity house, a dormitory, or a saloon. On the debit side, it may be said that fraternities—and, of course, sororities—emphasize external possessions such as money, and trivialities such as appearances or "family." Their tradition of snobbishness inflates the ego of ordinary individuals who "make" them and too often breaks the hearts of those who do not. Fraternities are neither a menace nor a boon, and parents and students would both be better off if they regarded them as unimportant.

I have never been a college athlete, but I have been a soldier, and as soldiery and athletics demand much the same things of a young man, I feel qualified to have some opinions on athletics. Moreover, I have attended many football games, addressed many athletic banquets, and examined many athletic budgets. The result of my contact with athletics is my conviction that athletics have a place in college, but only up to the point where they interfere with giving and getting an education. Many years ago, long before the football era was well under way, Thorstein Veblen said, "Football has no more to do with culture than bullfighting has to do with agriculture."

College should make a man manly. It can do this by developing his courage and perserverance in the realms of thought. Just as much courage, and courage of a higher sort, is required to tackle a 200-pound idea as to tackle a 200-pound fullback. As long as athletics is recreation, it will do neither the student nor the college any harm and may do them good. When it becomes the chief interest of the student and a major source of income for the college, it will prevent the student from getting an education and the college from giving one. A college which subsidizes athletes as such degrades its educational efforts. A college which is interested in producing professional athletes is not an educational institution.

Some three hundred college and university presidents recently answered a questionnaire in which they were asked to list, in the order of importance, what they regarded as the purposes of their institutions. Mental discipline, which ranked first sixty years ago, according to a recent analysis of the college catalogues of that day, now ranks twenty-second among the twenty-five avowed purposes of our institutions of higher learning. It is preceded by such objects of higher education as good manners. "Good manners" have no place in the program of higher education. "Personality" has no place in the program of higher education. "Character" has no place in the program of higher education. College develops character by giving young people the habits of hard work and honest analysis. If it tries to teach character directly, it succeeds only in being boring.

An expensively dressed lady once approached the head of a school where I was a teacher and said, "My boy is eighteen years old, and I'm afraid he has been spoiled. I want you to take him and make a man out of him." The head of the school, who was one of the nation's wisest educators, lifted a line from the classics by way of reply: "Late, late, too late—ye cannot enter now."

Why, then, go to college? If the social graces and athletic proficiency can be obtained elsewhere and for less money, if it is too late to alter profoundly the character of a boy or girl of eighteen, perhaps the reason for going to college is to learn how to get into the higher income tax brackets.

This is the reason why a large proportion of our young people go to college. This is one of the reasons why the colleges and universities of the United States provide every imaginable type of specialized course. The thought of the colleges in offering specialized education instead of general education is that any student, by being submitted to imitations of experiences he may have in later life, will be able to make a million dollars by repeating those experiences in the outside world.

The student who has had a general education, who has mastered the fundamental principles of the sciences and the arts, can adjust himself to the world. He can acquire specific techniques in a few weeks or a few months. A college graduate who has concerned himself with the whole field of physics and has achieved an understanding of the relation of the ideas that underlie physics need not worry about getting a job if television should suddenly become a major industry. Nor need he worry if television is replaced by something else.

To this extent college education helps a student earn a living. To this extent it prepares him for the unpredictable variety of unpredictable experiences with which he may be confronted. College is not the place to learn how to make a million dollars, although it will help a student to earn a living by teaching him to use his head, and to use it on whatever problems may confront him.

College is a place to learn how to think. A college graduate who has not learned how to think may make a million dollars, but he will have wasted his time going to college.

I have not been able to discover that the present college generation is much different from my own. We are told that times are different since the crash of 1929. We are told that a new seriousness is sweeping the colleges. The old campus policeman, who has seen generations of them come and go, is quoted as observing that college students are wearing frowns and even scowls. He is quoted as complaining that the red lamp over the open manhole has not been stolen for several years now.

Perhaps he is right, I, too, have observed, like the old policeman, that the students are not so frivolous as I was. But I am not convinced that the new seriousness is meritorious in itself. It is not so important to be serious as it is to be serious about important things. The monkey wears an expression of seriousness which would do credit to any college student, but the monkey is serious because he itches. The depression, which is credited with having brought on the new seriousness in the colleges, merely intensified the conviction of students and their parents that it is important to make money. The new seriousness is a seriousness about the financial future of the individual, reflected in his determination to get some kind of training that will guarantee him what he calls security.

For decades people have been writing articles to show that college graduates make more money than their fellow men. This pious hope is more vehemently expressed today than ever before. As long as our people cling to the illusion that nothing is as important as making money, our colleges and universities will continue to try to teach young people how to make money. They will try to be what we want them to be. They will try to do what we insist they do. And they will fail to give youth the one thing it can get nowhere else, and that is an intellect rigorously trained for the happiness of the individual and the salvation of the world.

At the risk of lapsing into my Commencement Oration manner, I want to suggest that if the goal of life is happiness, you who are going to college should seek the training of the intellect. I repeat: If the goal of life is happiness, you should seek the training of the intellect. Does this sound meaningless? Do you doubt that happiness and the intellect have anything to do with each other?

A trained intellect may increase your earning capacity. On the other hand, it may not. But this it will do—it will provide you with the joy of understanding. And if you have understanding, you will have character. For you cannot be good without being wise. You cannot be right without knowing what is right and what is wrong.

Character, even if it is well grounded by the habits and conventions of early life, may collapse in later years if understanding is not present to support it. For as you grow older you will confront corrupting influences. You will confront "easy" ways to make money and "easy" ways to drown your sorrows. Against such pressures as these, habits and conventions will not prevail unless your reason convinces you that they should.

Nor can you be wise without being good. Your wisdom will enable you to select the means by which you may attain the ends you seek. If you seek the wrong ends, you may turn out to be a wise murderer. Since it is not wise to be a murderer, not even a wise murderer, you will recognize the impossibility of trying to be wise without being good. One of the reasons our age is bewildered and unmoral is that we have tried to separate wisdom and goodness.

So you will want both understanding and character. Some of our people believe, or at least live as if they believed, that it is not understanding and character which determines happiness but the external possessions one acquires, such as money, fame, and power. They believe that happiness can be bought. I submit that it cannot.

In the first place, there is no sure way to get money, fame, and power. They are goods of chance. Hence, while any man who wants them will work as hard as possible, any man who has attained them must admit that his success may be largely an accident. The accidents of birth, location, and friendship have led more men to wealth and glory than the practice of the virtues. Many of the men whose lives serve as examples to succeeding generations lived poor and died penniless.

As there is no sure way to get these possessions, so there is no sure way to keep them.

In our own time we have seen fortunes, reputations, and thrones swept away overnight. You may lose these possessions through no fault of your own. No one blames the people who lost their savings in the recent depression. Most of these people worked hard and were honest. Yet they lost their possessions.

But even if you are lucky enough to get these things and keep them, they will become monotonous. You will get tired of too many houses and too much food. Some of the wealthiest people in the world are bored. I have known rich men who were so bored that they even wanted to be college professors.

The possession of beautiful things does not in itself guarantee their enjoyment. There is small choice between the man who owns a library and the man who cannot afford a book, if neither of them appreciates literature. Monotony overtakes them both.

Finally, when you have dedicated your lives to the acquisition of money, fame, and power, you have become the slaves of insatiable masters. Some men say, "Let me make a lot of money, then I will turn to higher things." I have known many such men, and they never lived long enough to turn to higher things, although some of them lived very long.

The question that was asked twenty-five hundred years ago is still unanswerable: "How can that be wealth of which a man may have a great abundance and yet perish with hunger, like Midas in the fable, whose insatiable prayer turned everything that was set before him into gold?"

If the goal of life is happiness and if you cannot buy happiness, you will seek it in wisdom and goodness. You will willingly surrender the goods outside of you for the goods of the mind and the goods of the character. These are the main constituents of any abiding happiness. These alone survive every change of fortune. These alone can be won and retained by any man.

You can devote yourselves to the virtues of the mind and the character and still lead a satisfying, even an exciting life. There is no monotony in the world of the mind and the character. Here the variety of possible experiences is unlimited. Books, people, places take on meaning for you. You will live on a more complex, and, therefore, more interesting level. You can converse with your fellow men, and, since there is no end of ideas in the world, conversation will never pall. You will be able to solve your problems and you will be able to have peace.

I have said that these goods differ from external goods in that they can be won and retained by any man. The future holds out the promise of increasing time for leisure, so that the man who in the past has been too tired at the end of the day to do anything but sleep or go to the movies will have the time and the energy to develop his mind. When you have these things you can never lose them. They are not listed on the stock exchanges. You cannot be sold out.

Marcus Aurelius said: "Understand that a man is worth just so much as the things are worth about which he busies himself." If you busy yourself only with animal comforts, you will not know the dignity and importance of being a man. You may be only as happy as the most contented cow. Only if you busy yourself with the affairs of the mind and the spirit will you know the higher happiness of the creature which differs from the rest of the beasts.

College education in the United States is still restricted to a fraction of the nation's young people. It falls short of providing even that fraction with the understanding which produces the moral and intellectual excellence which, in turn, is the mark of a free man and a free people. A nation which cherishes the freedom of its citizens will try to give all its children an education. It will try to give them the kind of education that leads to understanding.

why go to college

1. Which of the following best fits the definition of an *educated* college student?
   - a. he is a bright self-supporting student
   - b. he has disciplined mental powers
   - c. he gets good grades in spite of extracurricular activities
   - d. he is well-informed on various subjects
2. Why is the student confused at the beginning of his college life?
   - a. he is not yet adjusted to his new environment

    b. he has always been just an average student

    c. his previous schooling has not adequately prepared him for college

    d. the courses in college are so different from those he had taken in high school

3. What purpose is served by referring to the way some students spend their college life as "treading a weary round, picking up a fragment here and a fragment there?"

    a. it indirectly ridicules the uncritical acquisition of facts without ever integrating them

    b. it implies that college life can be dull if one does not take advantage of a non-academic activity here and there

    c. it subtly mocks those students who, bored with college, just take a course or two that they like

    d. it suggests that one goes through college as a matter of routine, picking up an idea here and there

4. The over-all pattern of development in this selection is one of contrast. The differences being pointed out are between:

    a. the American college system and foreign ones

    b. self-supporting bright students and average ones

    c. going to college and getting an education in college

    d. American educational ideals in the 20's and those at present

5. Which of the following words is emotive?

    a. as you grow older you will confront *corrupting* influences

    b. some of the wealthiest people in the world are *bored*

    c. you can lead a satisfying, even an *exciting* life

    d. our age is *bewildered* and unmoral

6. Which of the following best describes the tone of this passage?

    a. argumentative and expository with an underlying didactic intent

    b. humorous and argumentative with an underlying satirical intent

    c. expository and cynical with an underlying didactic intent

    d. descriptive and humorous with an underlying satirical intent

7. Which of the following best describes the moral or philosophical attitude expressed in this selection?

    a. to deprive a qualified person of a college education is an offense against the individual and society

    b. getting a college education is a serious business of developing one's moral and mental excellences

    c. "a man is worth just so much as the things are worth about which he busies himself"

    d. fame, money, and power are insatiable masters that often lead to unhappiness

8. Which of the following inferences seems most likely as a description of the author's attitude regarding the place of extracurricular activities in college?

    a. he believes that extracurricular activities are valuable in the social development of the student

b. he favors certain extracurricular activities such as athletics and condemns others such as fraternities

c. he believes that extracurricular activities have no place in a reputable university or college

d. he discourages emphasizing extracurricular activities at the expense of developing the mind and character

9. What purpose is served by the author's referring to the college life of students who are not getting an education as "an unrippled stream"?

    a. it emphasizes the peacefulness of such a life

    b. it suggests that such a life has no problems

    c. it calls attention to the lack of challenge in such a life

    d. it implies that there is no excitement in such a life

10. Which of the following best describes the author's intention in this selection?

    a. he is indirectly pleading for a re-assessment of educational values

    b. he is suggesting a return to the educational ideals of the past

    c. he is indirectly satirizing the colleges and the students of today

    d. he is indirectly indicting the materialism of the present

2

comments

Five Bewildered Freshman

Professor Carl Becker, Cornell's great teacher and historian, puts forth in a most informal manner the best orientation to college that I have ever read.

For some students, this discussion may make the difference between staying in college or leaving. I have known students who had voluntarily withdrawn because college was not what they thought it would be. They were mainly disturbed by what seemed to them random discussion of topics by both students and professors. No doubt, they had expected that the learned professor, as sage and master, would pour forth facts and immutable truths. Such students could have been saved, I am sure, if they had realized that education is a quest for knowledge by both student and professor.

Other students, who plan to remain the four years no matter what, will be helped since this letter will provide them with an indispensable point of view. They will henceforth try to assemble and reassemble what they read, hear, and discuss in a form that makes sense to them. They will not wait for someone to impose order miraculously on the random heap. Those who wait will miss the opportunity for an education.

Five Bewildered Freshmen

Carl Becker

ONE I was interested in the letter of Five Bewildered Freshmen, and in the discussion it gave rise to. The freshmen say they have been engaged in the intellectual life for more than two months and don't know what it's all about. This is bad, but who is to blame? Some say the students are to blame, and some say the professors. What is to be done about it? You suggest a foundation or an orientation course such as is given in other universities.

TWO For my part, I don't blame anyone—not the freshmen, certainly. It's not especially the student's fault if he doesn't know what it's all about. If he did, he wouldn't need to come to college. That's why, I have always supposed, young people come to college—to get some notion, even if only a glimmering, of what it's about. They come to get "oriented." But why expect to be oriented in two months, or a year? The whole four-year college course is a course in orientation. It isn't a very satisfactory one, indeed. Four years isn't enough. Life itself is scarcely long enough to enable one to find out what it's all about.

THREE Neither do I blame the professors—not particularly. Many people appear to think that professors possess some secret of knowledge and wisdom which would set the students right as to the meaning of things if they would only impart it. This, I do assure you, is an illusion. I could write you a letter on behalf of Five Bewildered Professors which would make the five bewildered freshmen appear cocksure by comparison. The professors are in the same boat. They don't know either what it's all about. They tried to find out when in college, and they have been trying ever since. Most of them, if they are wise, don't expect ever to find out, not really. But still they will, if they are wise, keep on trying. That is, indeed, just what the intellectual life is—a continuous adventure of the mind in which something is being discovered possessing whatever meaning the adventurer can find in it.

FOUR This effort to find out what it's all about is, in our time, more difficult than ever before. The reason is that the old foundations of assured faith and familiar custom are crumbling under our feet. For

This article appeared as a letter by Professor Becker in answer to one which had previously appeared in the columns of the newspaper. Reprinted by permission of the *Cornell Daily Sun*.

four hundred years the world of education and knowledge rested securely on two fundamentals which were rarely questioned. These were *Christian philosophy* and *Classical learning*. For the better part of a century Christian faith has been going by the board, and Classical learning into the discard. To replace these we have as yet no foundations, no certainties. We live in a world dominated by machines, a world of incredibly rapid change, a world of naturalistic science and of physico-chemico-libido psychology. There are no longer any certainties either in life or in thought. Everywhere confusion. Everywhere questions. Where are we? Where did we come from? Where do we go from here? What is it all about? The freshmen are asking, and they may well ask. Everyone is asking. No one knows; and those who profess with most confidence to know are most likely to be mistaken. Professors could reorganize the College of Arts if they knew what a College of Arts should be. They could give students a "general education" if they knew what a general education was, or would be good for if one had it. Professors are not especially to blame because the world has lost all certainty about these things.

FIVE   One of the sure signs that the intellectual world is bewildered is that everywhere, in colleges and out, people are asking for "Orientation" courses which will tell the freshmen straight off what it is all about. If we were oriented we shouldn't need such courses. This does not mean that I am opposed to an orientation course for freshmen. I would like an orientation course for freshmen. I would like one for seniors. I would like one for professors and trustees. I would like one for President Farrand and President Butler. Only, who is to give it? And what is it to consist of? I asked Professor Hayes, "What about your orientation course at Columbia?" He said, "It's a good thing for the Instructors who give it." I asked a man whose son had taken the course, "What did he get out of it?" The reply was, "He read three books in three unrelated fields of knowledge and got a kick out of one of them." Who knows the "background" or the "general field of knowledge"? If the course is given by many professors, the student will be taking several courses as one course instead of several courses as separate courses. If one man gives it what will it be? It will be as good as the man is. If we could get a really topnotch man to give a course, no matter what, and call it an orientation course, I should welcome it. H. G. Wells might give such a course, and it would be a good course. I doubt if it would orient any one or settle anything, but it would stir the students up and make them think. That would be its great merit. That is the chief merit of any course—that it unsettles students, makes them ask questions.

SIX   The Five Bewildered Freshmen have got more out of their course than they know. It has made them ask a question—What is it all about? That is a pertinent question. I have been asking it for thirty-five years, and I am still as bewildered as they are.

five bewildered freshmen

1. From the context, which of the following definitions is best for the word *cocksure*? (Par. 3: "I could write you a letter on behalf of Five Bewildered Professors which would make the five bewildered freshmen appear *cocksure* by comparison.")

   a. uncertain
   b. confused
   c. quite certain
   d. trustworthy

2. Which of the following was the basis of education for four hundred years?

   a. an intellectual life
   b. Christian philosophy and classical learning
   c. naturalistic science and physico-chemico-libido psychology
   d. common sense

3. What is the purpose of referring to the "Five Bewildered Freshmen" and the "Five Bewildered Professors?"

   a. it implies professors are not well educated
   b. it implies that education does not end bewilderment
   c. it implies that people are forever bewildered
   d. it implies that education leads to further bewilderment and discovery

4. Which of the following phrases best describes the pattern of development of this passage?

   a. description of the parts of a whole
   b. a statement supported by several examples
   c. description of a situation that leads to a conclusion
   d. examples and comments about them

5. Which of the following words is used by Becker in an emotive sense?

   a. crumbling   (Par. 4: "The reason is that the old foundations of assured faith and familiar custom are *crumbling* under our feet.")
   b. questioned   (Par. 4: "For four hundred years the world of education and knowledge rested securely on two fundamentals which were rarely *questioned*.")
   c. blame   (Par. 1: "This is bad, but who is to *blame*.")
   d. incredibly   (Par. 4: "We live in a world dominated by machines, a world of *incredibly* rapid change. . . .")

6. Which of the following best describes the tone of this passage?

   a. rhetorical and descriptive
   b. descriptive with an underlying philosophical purpose
   c. rhetorical and argumentative
   d. impersonal and satirical

7. Which of the following best describes the moral or philosophical attitude expressed in this selection?

  a. an intellectual life leads to futile confusion
  b. questioning is the basis of an intellectual life
  c. one can resolve bewilderment through education
  d. one can find identity through an intellectual life

8. Which of the following inferences seems to reflect Becker's attitude toward H. G. Wells?

  a. he is the only person who "knows what it's all about"
  b. he leads an intellectual life
  c. he can stimulate students to continue questioning
  d. he can end the students' bewilderment

9. What purpose is served by Becker's listing the types of orientation courses he would recommend?

  a. to show that everyone has unanswered questions and needs orientation
  b. to show the number of people who would benefit from an orientation course
  c. to show the variety of courses offered in college
  d. to show the confusion in the world

10. Which of the following best describes the author's intention?

  a. he is arguing that college orientation is inadequate
  b. he is speaking against any type of orientation course for freshmen
  c. he is pointing out that only a few people in the world are qualified to teach orientation
  d. he is showing that the outcome of orientation should be uncertainty and questioning

part ii

On Scholarly Attitudes

Many freshman are unnecessarily confused about the tug between studies and college life. The problem not only revolves around an "either-or" argument, but around emphasis as well. The following two articles, by outstanding authorities, deal specifically with the interesting questions of: (a) college experience vs. academic studies; and (b) studying for facts or for principles.

3

comments

Academic Involvement

You will hear much talk about the value of a college experience. Students will actually say, "Whom you know and what fraternity you belong to are more important than courses and professors." And to "prove the argument" they will point to Jim, who was, in fact, a popular fellow, a fraternity man, and on the newspaper staff. The omission to mention that Jim was a scholar as well always leads the listeners to believe that Jim barely "squeeked" through academically.

The failure to mention his scholarship makes all the difference in the world. The picture becomes a big, smiling, well-dressed Jim, whose activities and interests revolved around friends, fraternity, and good living. Such a picture is a myth, for no one who totally neglects his studies can stay around a college campus long enough to establish such a one-sided record.

Actually, Jim existed, but here is the missing part: Jim was primarily a scholar. He studied hard; he never cut classes; his instructors thought highly of him; his grades were high enough to gain entrance to an outstanding medical school.

So here is the full picture: Jim made academic achievement the "sun" of his college life. Friends, fraternity, and activities were the satellites—important satellites.

A student who tries to make the "college experience" the center of his college universe will be able to say these sad words, "Yes, if I had stayed on for the other three years, I would have graduated with the class of '68."

I do not want to sound moralistic, but I have seen this happen too often to remain silent. If you don't want to utter the words "could have been," you must make studying your primary concern in college. If you do, then the creation of wonderful memories of college will be possible.

Academic Involvement

Percy Marks

ONE   Men commonly say that they learn more out of the classroom than in it, that "college life" in the end proves the real teacher. Usually the men who make that statement are entirely sincere, but they rarely reveal how much interest they took with them to the classroom and how capable intellectually they were of receiving anything from it. I know of one dean who always tells the incoming freshmen that they are in college for one great purpose and that purpose is to study. He is right, but only half right! Study is not an end in itself, a good in itself. No, you are going to college for something greater than study, of which study is only a part. Most of the men who received more from "college life" than they did in the classroom recognized the fact that study alone could not give them all the fruits of college, but they did not recognize the equally important fact that study was a ladder on which they could climb to the highest part of the academic tree, where the most luscious fruits grow. Really, the distinction that I have just made between college life and study is an anomaly; rightly considered, study is the richest, the most delightful part of college life.

Two   Most of you will not believe that statement. You will say: "Ah, there the pedagogue speaks!" Perhaps, I believe deeply in the truth of my assertion, nevertheless; and I believe in it so deeply because I have seen it proved many times. Once, for example, a boy came to me and told me that he was thinking of leaving college.

THREE   "I'm not learning a thing," he protested, "and I'm bored stiff. I'm getting so that I cut all the time, and I might just as well quit because I'm going to get flunked out if I don't."

FOUR   He was by no means a dullard, and he was magnificently honest; he confessed that he had sucked college life dry by his sophomore year, and now in the beginning of it, he was hanging on miserably to

Percy Marks, *Which Way Paranassus?* (New York: Harcourt, Brace & World, Inc., 1926). Copyright, 1926, by Harcourt Brace & World, Inc., renewed 1954, by Percy Marks. Reprinted by permission of the publisher.

the scarlet fringe; in other words, he was dissipating violently. I asked him if he had ever given his studies a chance, and he asked me what I meant.

FIVE "Well," I explained, "you seem to be one of the ninety-and-nine who expect something for nothing. You expect to enjoy your classes without bringing either interest or effort to them. You don't study; you cut regularly; and by your own confession, when you do go, you slump supinely on the back of your neck and dare the instructor to interest you. Well, nobody is going to take you by your little hand and kiss the delight of learning into you. Have you noticed that while you may be bored in every course, there are fellows who are deeply interested, and that while you find it impossible to sit down and study, there are fellows who are actually eager to get to their books?"

SIX He confessed that he had noticed the phenomenon but that he had made no effort to explain it.

SEVEN "You are getting nothing from your courses," I continued, "because you are taking less to them, and you aren't going to get much fun out of anything in this life by sprawling in an easy chair and moaning that life isn't interesting. If you were stupid, I'd tell you to quit college in a minute, both for your own good and the good of the college; but you aren't stupid, and there is no reason why you should not find both pleasure and profit in your studies. Why not give them at least a sporting chance? Why not try studying for a while? Who knows? You might find it an interesting experience; at least it will be something different."

EIGHT The novelty of the idea seemed to appeal to him. After two weeks of studying, he told me with grumbling resentment that he was working like a fool trying to catch up and that if I thought he was getting any thrills, I was a naïve child. I replied that he was the naïve child, since he so ingenuously expected to make up for past sins, carry on with the class, and create new interest at the same time. It took him a few weeks to realize that mere regret and new-found good intentions will not compensate for past laziness and ignorant guilt. In less than two months, however, he confessed to real pleasure in his work, and by the end of the term he was actually excited about it. He never lost the excitement, furthermore, and graduated with his class, proud of what he had learned and eager to learn more. That man will testify, I know, in any court that his most delightful activity was study and that the cream of college life is in becoming acquainted not with one's fellows, many of whom are dull clods, but with the greatest who have ever lived.

NINE And that, you know, is what studying is: getting acquainted with the wisest, the wittiest, the most delightful people who have ever walked this earth. The instructor is merely a go-between, an introducer. To all intents and purposes all that he does is say: "Gentlemen, my students: I wish to present to you William Shakespeare. He has a great deal to tell you, and he can tell it more delightfully, more beautifully, than any man speaking or writing the English language. He will make you laugh until your sides ache. He has a story about Prince Hal and John Falstaff so funny that I warn you here and now to hang on to any loose buttons. He has a story about a Moor named Othello who loved not wisely but too well; it is dramatic, it is tender, it is passionate. You will weep, and you will be better for the weeping. So, too, will you weep when he tells you about Prince Hamlet. There is so much of Hamlet in each of you that you will feel that he is telling your story, too; your inner story, I mean. Gentlemen, my students: William Shakespeare, the most poetic, the most dramatic, the most superb storyteller in the world."

TEN   No one can teach you Shakespeare so well as Shakespeare can, no one can teach you science as Huxley can, and no one can teach you philosophy as Plato can; but you might never hear of Shakespeare, Huxley, and Plato if your instructor did not tell you all about them. The great dead are shy, hiding all their wisdom and poetry, the wisdom and poetry of the world, in the quiet of college campuses. They do not walk the streets, slapping Tom, Dick, and Harry on the back, handing them carelessly their precious treasures, so long sought for, so tenderly labored over. Only the earnest can meet them, only the humble can win their love, only the zealous can find the way to their treasure house. The instructor is a guide, waiting to show you the road. He may be a poor guide, leading you blindly by the hand, but if he is willing, if he is eager to lead, do not scorn his help. Together you may find something inestimably precious.

academic involvement

1. From the context, which of the following definitions is best for the word, *phenomenon?* (Par. 6: "He confessed that he had noticed the *phenomenon* but that he had made no effort to explain it.")
   a. an event of unique significance
   b. any object known through the senses rather than through thought or intuition
   c. occurrence
   d. abnormal thing

2. The boy was getting nothing from his courses because:
   a. he was a dullard
   b. the courses were not interesting
   c. he had sucked college life dry by his sophomore year
   d. he brought neither interest nor effort to his classes

3. What purpose is served by the following figure of speech? (Par. 1: ". . . study was a ladder on which they could climb to the highest part of the academic tree, where the most luscious fruits grow.")

    a. to clarify the author's distinction between study and "college life"

    b. to explain the relation between study and "college life"

    c. to impress upon the reader the equal importance of study and "college life"

    d. to prepare the reader for the author's conception of study "rightly considered"

4. Which of the following phrases best describes the pattern of development of this selection?

    a. refutation of an anomaly through example

    b. example and comment lead to definition of study

    c. omniscient author technique

    d. the author relates a conversation to prove the truth of his point of view

5. Which of the following words is *not* used in an emotive sense?

a. dissipating violently	(Par. 4: ". . . he was *dissipating violently*.")
b. past sins	(Par. 8: "I replied that he was the naïve child, since he so ingenuously expected to make up for *past sins*.")
c. pleasure and profit	(Par. 7: ". . . there is no reason why you should not find both *pleasure and profit* in your studies.")
d. novelty	(Par. 8: "The *novelty* of the idea seemed to appeal to him.")

6. Which of the following best describes the tone of this selection?

    a. serious and argumentative

    b. humorous but moralistic

    c. satirical with an underlying irony

    d. logical and impersonal

7. Which of the following best describes the moral or philosophical attitude expressed in the first paragraph?

    a. a distinction between study and "college life" is an anomaly

    b. "college life" in the end proves the real teacher

    c. study is an end in itself

    d. study is the richest, most delightful part of college life

8. Which of the following inferences seems most likely as a description of the author's attitude toward study when he says, ". . . there is no reason why you should not find both pleasure and profit in your studies."

    a. study is a means to entertainment and material gains

    b. the intellectual and spiritual rewards of earnest study are invaluable

    c. pleasure and profit are the rewards for diligence

    d. what you get out of something depends on what you put into it

9. What purpose is served by the elaboration of names in the last paragraph: "No one can teach you Shakespeare so well as Shakespeare can . . . science as Huxley can . . . but you might never hear of Shakespeare Huxley, and Plato if your instructor did not tell you all about them."

a. to praise the instructors

b. it enables him to illustrate how the dramatic technique can be employed in a classroom situation

c. to indicate some of the steps on the ladder to the most luscious fruit on the academic tree

d. it enables him to illustrate the variety and interest that the ordinary person can obtain from reading Shakespeare

10. Which of the following best describes the author's intention in this passage?

a. to prove that study is more important than "college life"

b. to prove to the boy that there was no reason why he should not find pleasure and profit in study

c. to define study and its part in college life

d. to bemoan the fact that "ninety-and-nine" people expect something for nothing

4

comments

Purpose and Concentration

In this paper the author sets up a relationship between study for facts and principles, and study to discipline the mind. Though he emphasizes the disciplining of the mind he does not relegate the studying for facts to an unimportant place, and rightly so.

The author realisticly assumes that man must know many specific facts to deal with other men and with his environment efficiently and effectively. Only recently I heard a factual account of an amazing experience of a colleague working on an educational project in Liberia. This man, while walking in the nearby forest, suddenly found himself entangled in the coils of a huge python which fell upon him from an overhanging branch. Feeling the pressure of the constricting coils, he immediately began searching his mind for a solution. He remembered reading somewhere that a gentle tickling of a python's underside with the finger produces a relaxing effect. The fact that he is still working at his job in Liberia attests to the effectiveness of this procedure.

Neither I nor the author is suggesting that one should fill his mind with odd bits of information, but we do urge that as one pursues an academic career by studying, reading, listening, reflecting, he should make a determined effort to retain as much specific information as he can while attempting to understand the principles and laws underlying such data.

Purpose and Concentration

Francis C. Lockwood

ONE   What are the real aims of study? The object of study is, in the
first place, to get fast and firm possession of facts—facts of spelling, reading, mathematics, composition, history, language, geography, and the
like. It is highly desirable that we should know how to spell *Chicago*
and *business; Boston* and *brains;* and that we should know for all time.
We want to know once for all that seven times nine are sixty-three;
that Abraham Lincoln signed the Emancipation Proclamation; that an
island is a body of land completely surrounded by water; and that a
proper name should begin with a capital letter. Many, many, minute
facts, as well as certain connected bodies of truth, should be embedded
in one's memory as deeply and securely as a bullet that has lodged in
the heart of a growing tree. And one should master certain processes of
thought, and grip a few great underlying and unchanging principles of
life and conduct.

Two   Yet the chief value of study does not lie in the stowing away
of facts and principles. You study for discipline. You study in order that
you may become a student, just as you exercise, not for recreation alone,
but that you may become an athlete. In making yourself a student you
are making yourself fit for the fierce intellectual encounters of middle
life. No time for training then! And woe to him whose brainfiber is
flabby then, whose mental processes are slow and hazy and uncertain!
Your mind must work with the force and steadiness of a piston rod, must
clutch like a vise. You will be pitted against antagonists worthy of your
mettle. They will not sleep; nor will they let you sleep during the long
day of strain in the courtroom, on the stump, in the halls of legislation,
at the editorial desk, in the countinghouse, where the tides of traffic run
full and hot, and where masters of finance and captains of industry sit
secretly, silently, astutely making or marring your fortunes or the fortunes of weak men and women whose champion you are. It may be that
with knife or drug you will suddenly be set in the lonely night to hold
Death at bay in some terrified home, or on some tragic highway or byway.
You are winning these crucial contests now by the precision and the
promptness and the thoroughness that you are working into your higher

Francis C. Lockwood, *The Freshman and His College* (Boston: D. C. Heath &
Company, 1913).

nerve centers; by the severe training that you are giving yourself in attention, decision, mental alertness, and moral control.

THREE Again, it is worth while to study because there is nothing in the world so glorious as truth, nothing so fascinating as the pursuit of wisdom. Mind alone can unlock the meaning of the world. If we would be free we must think ourselves free. To the degree that we are ignorant we are slaves—slaves to wind and wave, to time and tide, to sin and pain, to man and devil and microbe. But to the extent that we study and think and gain wisdom, we drive back the barriers of darkness and come into the full freedom of our own free spirits. There is in us a divine curiosity that urges us to perpetual inquiry. We are set in this world to solve riddles. We study because there burns within us an unquenched and unquenchable passion to uncover reality; to drive out the bogies and the fetishes and the hoodoos that lurk in this human wilderness through which we are traveling. Study purifies and exalts the student. It loosens the bonds of Time and Space. Study enthrones a man with the gods. Through study we may escape into the infinite and the eternal; we may unite ourselves with God.

FOUR Study consists in focusing the mind upon the subject in hand. In very early life we have almost no power of voluntary attention; and even the mature scholar can hold his mind on a given object only for an instant by his own will power. The little child scarcely has any mind that he can call his own. He lives out of doors, on the open highways of sensation. His mind is snatched hither and thither by the bright baubles and the entrancing sounds around him. He surrenders himself completely and on the spot to the last and gaudiest attraction that bids for his attention. We laugh at professors and philosophers for being absent-minded. In reality they are not absent-minded at all; they are so *present-minded* that they are utterly oblivious of their bodies and of everything around them. They have learned the art of study, and are giving attention mightily.

FIVE With children—and with many college students—it is exactly the opposite. Their bodies are chained to the tasks before them, but their minds are absent on other and more attractive pursuits. Now the trouble with many students is that they are still children. They have never learned how to hold their attention closely and sternly to a set task. They are given to dawdling and to idle daydreaming. They are at the mercy of every sensation and every enticement. An educated person learns "to do the thing he does not want to do, at the time he does not want to do it."

SIX In the long run the secret of study resides in our ability to bathe our thought, our task, our lesson in the stream of interest. The way to study successfully and joyously is to be interested in the thing that claims our attention. It is not hard to interest a boy in a dog, or a gun, or a swimming hole. Dress and travel and baseball and automobiles and dinner parties interest everyone. But how remote these things all seem from the stupid rules and theorems and outlines and repellent facts that we find staring at us from our textbooks, and forever tripping us up in the classroom!

SEVEN Yet, in reality, these two realms are not altogether removed from each other. There are connecting threads, if only we can find them. We must learn to carry over from the things that we do like, or the things that we are absorbed in, fragments or filaments of interest which may be attached to the dull or hated study that we must master. Of course the surest and most natural way to bring this about is to live such an alert, wide-awake, and sympathetic life that the world speaks our language at whatever point we accost it. It is well to have sensations and experiences and some slight information, at least, stored up from many sources. The greater our store of facts, images, experiences, and associations from the past, the more likely we are to find some point of contact between a new subject and an old one, and so to transfer interest from one to the other.

EIGHT If a subject seems hopelessly dry, one may approach it in some such way as this: It has interested other men; why should I be a stranger to it? Or, let one say to oneself: This subject, whatever its attractiveness or lack of attractiveness, is the sort of thing that comes to life out there in the world—the sort of thing that men are stumbling over on every human highway. What I study now is related to what I am going to do hereafter. Somewhere, sometime, in a moment of doubt, or need, or loneliness, or crisis, this little, hard, unattractive, apparently insignificant scrap of fact, bit of quotation, or statement of principle may saunter obligingly into my mind at need, and prove as welcome to me as would a comrade or a brother.

NINE One may study with the thought of future travel. "He that would bring home the wealth of the Indies must carry out the wealth of the Indies." That is, we shall see only what we are prepared to see. Study, with the thought of making yourself an interesting and resourceful conversationalist. Study, again, for the rewards of scholarship; or if this is no incentive, study in order to win honor for your "bunch," your fraternity, your family, your country.

TEN And study, finally, if no other interest serves, *because you are a man*. It is nonsense to suppose that every step in education *can* be interesting. The fighting impulse must often be appealed to. Be ashamed of being scared at fractions, of being downed by the law of falling bodies; rouse your pugnacity and pride, and you will rush at the difficult places with a sort of inner wrath at yourself that is one of your best moral faculties. A victory scored under such conditions becomes a turning point and a crisis of your character. It represents the high-water mark of your powers, and serves thereafter as an ideal pattern for your self-imitation.

purpose and concentration

1. From the context, which of the following definitions is best for the word *mettle?* (Par. 2: "You will be pitted against antagonists worthy of your *mettle.*")

     a. interference
     b. stamina
     c. spirit
     d. hardness

2. What is the chief value of study?

     a. for minute facts
     b. for connected bodies of truth
     c. for discipline
     d. for principles of life

3. What is the purpose of the simile in which the author stresses that certain basis facts "should be imbedded in one's memory as deeply and securely as a bullet that has lodged in the heart of a growing tree"?

     a. it implies that a kernel of truth is always necessary
     b. it exaggerates the need for keeping facts in mind
     c. it implies that one should make himself fit for the encounters of middle life
     d. it implies that certain facts form an indestructible core upon which ever-expanding layers of knowledge can be built

4. Which of the following phrases best describes the pattern of development of Paragraph 4?

     a. comparison and contrast
     b. development by particulars and details
     c. development by definition
     d. development by using an extended metaphor

5. Which of the following words from Paragraph 3 is used by Lockwood in an emotive sense?

     a. spirits   (". . . the full freedom of our own free *spirits.*")
     b. barriers   (". . . we drive back the *barriers* of darkness . . .")
     c. burns   ("We study because there *burns* within us an unquenched . . .")
     d. slaves   ("To the degree that we are ignorant we are *slaves* . . .")

6. Which of the following best describes the tone of the final paragraph?

     a. logical and impersonal
     b. moralistic and descriptive
     c. emotive and serious
     d. descriptive and argumentative

7. Which of the following best describes the moral or philosophical attitude expressed in the passage, (Par. 9) "He that would bring home the wealth of the Indies must carry out the wealth of the Indies."

a. wealth is available if we will travel for it
b. we see only what we are prepared to see
c. man should be free to travel and thus increase his knowledge
d. man must have the foresight to hire enough honest men to carry the wealth to the coast

8. Which of the following inferences seems most likely as a description of Lockwood's intent in the final paragraph?

a. he urges us to be angry with ourselves
b. he stresses that every step in education can be interesting
c. he implies that a victory over self tends to cultivate man's highest powers
d. he indicates that every turning point is a crisis of your character

9. In Paragraph 8, for what purpose does Lockwood describe "dry" subjects as "the sort of thing that men are stumbling over on every human highway"?

a. he means that life is a burden
b. he implies that the ability to do things we dislike is a key to success
c. he demonstrates that the classroom is a mirror of life
d. he suggests that we must store up information from many sources

10. In Paragraph 3, which of the following best describes the author's intention in the passage beginning: "Mind alone can unlock the meaning of the world."

a. he is arguing that man is naturally inquisitive
b. he is suggesting that we are slaves to sin and pain
c. he is indicating that the pursuit of wisdom will lead man out of the darkness of superstition and ignorance
d. he is urging an end to restrictive institutions

part iii

On Psychological Processes

Psychologists working in the area of learning have developed some exciting principles. Such principles, of course, are of little benefit unless you are aware of them, and understand how they can help you learn easier, faster, or more deeply.

In this section we have presented selections which should lay the mental groundwork for any student who aspires to do a good job academically.

5

comments

The Laws of Habit

In this article, William James brings us face to face with reality—the consequences of our every act. We are made to realize, like it or not, that every action of an individual is recorded in his nervous system and that his personal development is formed in this manner.

Every time a person says, "I'll do that tomorrow instead of today," or "I'll skip class this morning and grab some extra sleep," such actions do not thereby irrevocably make this student a confirmed proscrastinator nor a "class-skipper," but these very actions will help make the same behavior easier and more natural the next time.

Paradoxically, the person who says, "I want to be free. I don't want to be an automaton. I want to do things when I feel like doing them," is, in fact, on the road toward losing the very freedom he seeks by becoming an automaton of indecision, frustration, and chaos. Actually, the person who is most free, is the person who builds up self-discipline through proper, necessary, and repeated acts which become so automatic that he is, in fact, free to be free.

Again, we have William James, whose keen insight into human nature and genuine interest in man helps man help himself.

The Laws of Habit

William James

ONE   All our life, so far as it has definite form, is but a mass of habits—
practical, emotional, and intellectual—systematically organized for our
weal or woe, and bearing us irresistibly toward our destiny, whatever
the latter may be. . . .

TWO   I believe that we are subject to the law of habit in consequence of the fact that we have bodies. The plasticity of the living matter
of our nervous system, in short, is the reason why we do a thing with
difficulty the first time, but soon do it more and more easily, and finally,
with sufficient practice, do it semi-mechanically, or with hardly any consciousness at all. Our nervous systems have *grown* to the way in which
they have been exercised, just as a sheet of paper or a coat, once creased
or folded, tends to fall forever afterward into the same identical folds. . . .

THREE   The great thing in all education is to *make our nervous
system our ally instead of our enemy.* It is to find and capitalize our
acquisitions, and live at ease upon the interest of the fund. *For this we
must make automatic and habitual, as early as possible, as many useful
actions as we can,* and as carefully guard against the growing into ways
that are likely to be disadvantageous. The more of the details of our
daily life we can hand over to the effortless custody of automatism, the
more our higher powers of mind will be set free for their own proper
work. There is no more miserable human being than one in whom nothing
is habitual but indecision, and for whom the lighting of every cigar, the
drinking of every cup, the time of rising and going to bed every day,
and the beginning of every bit of work are subjects of express volitional
deliberation. Fully half the time of such a man goes to the deciding or
regretting of matters which ought to be so ingrained in him as practically
not to exist for his consciousness at all. If there be such daily duties not
yet ingrained in any one of my hearers, let him begin this very hour to set
the matter right.

FOUR   In Professor Bain's chapter on "The Moral Habits" there
are some admirable practical remarks laid down. Two great maxims
emerge from the treatment. The first is that in the acquisition of a new
habit, or the leaving off of an old one, we must take care to *launch our-*

William James, *Psychology* (New York: Holt, Rinehart & Winston, Inc., 1893),
pp. 149–50. Reprinted by permission of the publisher.

selves with as strong and decided an initiative as possible. Accumulate all the possible circumstances which shall reinforce the right motives; put yourself assiduously in conditions that encourage the new way; make engagements incompatible with the old; take a public pledge, if the case allows; in short, envelope your resolution with every aid you know. This will give your new beginning such a momentum that the temptation to break down will not occur as soon as it otherwise might; and every day during which a breakdown is postponed adds to the chances of its not occurring at all. . . .

FIVE   The second maxim is *never suffer an exception to occur till the new habit is securely rooted in your life.* Each lapse is like the letting fall of a ball of string which one is carefully winding up: a single slip undoes more than a great many turns will wind again. Continuity of training is the great means of making the nervous system act infallibly right. . . .

SIX   A third maxim may be added to the preceding pair: *Seize the very first possible opportunity to act on every resolution you make, and on every emotional prompting you may experience in the direction of the habits you aspire to gain.* It is not in the moment of their forming, but in the moment of their producing motor effects, that resolves and aspirations communicate the new "set" to the brain.

SEVEN   No matter how full a reservoir of maxims one may possess, and no matter how good one's sentiments may be, if one has not taken advantage of every concrete opportunity to act, one's character may remain entirely unaffected for the better. With good intentions, hell proverbially is paved. This is an obvious consequence of the principles I have laid down. A "character," as J. S. Mill says, "is a completely fashioned will"; and a will, in the sense in which he means it, is an aggregate of tendencies to act in a firm and prompt and definite way upon all the principal emergencies of life. A tendency to act only becomes effectively ingrained in us in proportion to the uninterrupted frequency with which the actions actually occur, and the brain "grows" to their use. When a resolve or a fine glow of feeling is allowed to evaporate without bearing practical fruit, it is worse than a chance lost: it works so as positively to hinder future resolutions and emotions from taking the normal path of discharge. There is no more contemptible type of human character than that of the nerveless sentimentalist and dreamer, who spends his life in a weltering sea of sensibility, but never does a concrete manly deed. . . .

EIGHT   As a final practical maxim, relative to these habits of the will, we may, then offer something like this: *Keep the faculty of effort alive in you by a little gratuitous exercise every day.* That is, be systematically ascetic or heroic in little unnecessary points, do every day or two something for no other reason than that you would rather not do it,

so that when the hour of dire need draws nigh, it may find you not
unnerved and untrained to stand the test. Asceticism of this sort is like
the insurance which a man pays on his house and goods. The tax does him
no good at the time, and possibly may never bring him a return. But if
the fire *does* come, his having paid it will be his salvation from ruin. So
with the man who has daily inured himself to habits of concentrated
attention, energetic volition, and self-denial in unnecessary things. He
will stand like a tower when everything rocks around him, and when his
softer fellow mortals are winnowed like chaff in the blast.

NINE   The physiological study of mental conditions is thus the most
powerful ally of hortatory ethics. The hell to be endured hereafter, of
which theology tells, is no worse than the hell we make for ourselves in
this world by habitually fashioning our characters in the wrong way.
Could the young but realize how soon they will become mere walking
bundles of habits, they would give more heed to their conduct while in
the plastic state. We are spinning our own fates, good or evil, and never
to be undone. Every smallest stroke of virtue or of vice leaves its never
so little scar. The drunken Rip Van Winkle, in Jefferson's play, excuses
himself for every fresh dereliction by saying, "I won't count this time!"
Well! he may not count it, and a kind Heaven may not count it; but it is
being counted none the less. Down among his nerve cells and fibres the
molecules are counting it, registering and storing it up to be used against
him when the next temptation comes. Nothing we ever do is, in strict
scientific literalness, wiped out. Of course this has its good side as well
as its bad one. As we become permanent drunkards by so many separate
drinks, so we become saints in the moral, and authorities and experts
in the practical and scientific spheres, by so many separate acts and hours
of work. Let no youth have any anxiety about the upshot of his education,
whatever the line of it may be. If he keep faithfully busy each hour of
the working day, he may safely leave the final result to itself. He can
with perfect certainty count on waking up some fine morning, to find
himself one of the competent ones of his generation, in whatever pursuit he may have singled out. Silently, between all the details of his
business, the *power of judging* in all that class of matter will have
built itself up within him as a possession that will never pass away.
Young people should know this truth in advance. The ignorance of it
has probably engendered more discouragement and faintheartedness in
youths embarking on arduous careers than all other causes put together.

the laws of habit

1. The "great thing" in all education is to:
    a. develop a system of semi-mechanical habits
    b. make our nervous system our ally instead of our enemy
    c. greet each new challenge with an individual set or pattern of reactions
    d. learn

2. Our acquired habits, according to the author:
    a. may be changed at will
    b. are stepping stones of our conditioning
    c. affect our fate
    d. are systematically organized

3. It is suggested that since we "create" our own "world"
    a. we should train young children to have only good habits and to beware of forming bad ones
    b. we should avoid having too many habits
    c. we should train only adults in the conscious formation of habits
    d. we can not train anyone to have certain habits, they just happen naturally

4. Which of the following phrases best describes the pattern of development of this passage?
    a. comparing and contrasting two ideas
    b. description of a situation with a conclusion
    c. examples followed by philosophical insight based on the examples
    d. makes a statement, comments on it, and reinforces it with examples

5. Which of the following words is used by the author in an emotive sense?
    a. plasticity (Par. 2: "The *plasticity* of the living matter of our nervous system . . .")
    b. ingrained (Par. 3: "If there be such daily duties not yet *ingrained* in any one of my hearers, let him begin this very hour to set the matter right.")
    c. tower (Par. 8: "He will stand like a *tower* when everything rocks around him . . .")
    d. hortatory (Par. 9: "The physiological study of mental conditions is thus the most powerful ally of *hortatory* ethics.")

6. Which of the following best describes the tone of the passage?
    a. instructional with an underlying challenge
    b. figurative and emotional
    c. descriptive and argumentative
    d. informative and descriptive

7. The "moral" for humanity, especially the young, which is developed in the essay can be summed up as:

  a. all that glitters is not gold
  b. "a rolling stone gathers no moss"
  c. a habit earned is a habit learned
  d. don't put off until tomorrow what you can do today

8. It is suggested that we be on guard against:
  a. making negative or incorrect responses
  b. "too early" education
  c. habitual indecision
  d. "the effortless custody of automation"

9. Two great maxims emerging from Professor Bain's work on "Moral Habit" are:
  a. (1) to acquire a new habit one must use definite and strong initiative
    (2) one must shed undesirable habits gradually
  b. (1) take a public pledge
    (2) re-establish each old habit by a positive response
  c. (1) one must not employ varied responses while attempting to establish a new habit
    (2) one must shed undesirable habits gradually
  d. (1) to acquire a new habit one must use definite and strong initiative
    (2) one must not deviate from the new habit pattern while it is being established

10. The author's theory is that:
  a. our nervous system establishes habits through repeated practice
  b. our nervous system establishes positive habits more readily than negative habits
  c. that our nervous system is plastic
  d. consciousness is present at all times

6

comments

The Energies of Men

How often I hear students say, "I always seem to run out of time and energy to do a good job on my school work."

Notice that time and energy are usually used together. As far as time is concerned, all of us, rich or poor, weak or strong, diligent or wastrel, receive the same amount—24 hours a day; we cannot do anything about time since there is no way to get more of it. We can, however, do something about the second entity: energy.

Energy, both mental and physical, seems to be the mark of great men, who are somehow able to accomplish so much more than ordinary men. You have probably read biographies hoping to find perhaps the secret, but such secrets are not stated because the great men themselves are probably unaware of what really makes the difference.

William James, along with countless others, has mused on the secret of a full life and has suggested an answer: mental energy. More important though, he has developed a method by which we can tap the huge reservoirs of mental energy which lie within each of us.

This one essay has done more than any other I have found to help students gain control over their own lives. Students both in engineering and in liberal arts have attested to the essay's inestimable value.

Just to forestall the comment that one can push himself to a breakdown by overdoing, I'd like to answer that breakdowns rarely occur because of overwork: breakdowns usually occur because of continuous worry which gains control of the individual. In the academic life there is much excess worry over unfinished work and work poorly done.

As you read this essay, remember that William James was not just an excellent psychologist, nor a great philosopher; but also a medical

43

doctor aware of the limits of the human body and mind. Added to this, he traveled widely and conversed with the great men of his day. He studied painting under some of the outstanding masters. You are, therefore, exposed to the wisdom of a great man who speaks from a broad as well as a deep experience.

The Energies of Men

William James

ONE   Everyone knows what it is to start a piece of work, either intellectual or muscular, feeling stale. . . . And everybody knows what it is to "warm up" to his job. The process of warming up gets particularly striking in the phenomenon known as "second wind." On usual occasions we make a practice of stopping an occupation as soon as we meet the first effective layer (so to call it) of fatigue. We have then walked, played, or worked "enough," so we desist. That amount of fatigue is an efficacious obstruction on this side of which our usual life is cast. But if an unusual necessity forces us to press onward, a surprising thing occurs. The fatigue gets worse up to a certain critical point, when gradually or suddenly it passes away, and we are fresher than before. We have evidently tapped a level of new energy masked until then by the fatigue-obstacle usually obeyed. There may be layer after layer of this experience. A third and a fourth "wind" may supervene. Mental activity shows the phenomenon as well as physical, and in exceptional cases we may find, beyond the very extremity of fatigue-distress, amounts of ease and power that we never dreamed ourselves to own—sources of strength habitually not taxed at all, because habitually we never push through the obstruction, never pass those early critical points.

TWO   For many years I have mused on the phenomenon of second wind, trying to find a physiological theory. It is evident that our organism has stored-up reserves of energy that are ordinarily not called upon, but that may be called upon: deeper and deeper strata of combustible or explosible material, discontinuously arranged, but ready for use by anyone who probes so deep, and repairing themselves by rest as well as

William James, *On Vital Reserves* (New York: Holt, Rinehart & Winston, Inc., 1911), pp. 1–25. Reprinted by permission of the publisher.

do the superficial strata. Most of us continue living unnecessarily near our surface. . . .

THREE Of course there are limits: the trees don't grow into the sky. But the plain fact remains that men the world over possess amounts of resource which only very exceptional individuals push to their extremes of use. But the very same individual, pushing his energies to their extreme, may in a vast number of cases keep the pace up day after day, and find no "reaction" of a bad sort, so long as decent hygienic conditions are preserved. His more active rate of energizing does not wreck him; for the organism adapts itself, and as the rate of waste augments, augments correspondingly the rate of repair. . . .

FOUR If my reader will put together these two conceptions, first, that few men live at their maximum of energy, and second, that anyone may be in vital equilibrium at very different rates of energizing, he will find, I think, that a very pretty practical problem of national economy, as well as of individual ethics, opens upon his view. In rough terms, we may say that a man who energizes below his normal maximum fails by just so much to profit by his chance at life; and that a nation filled with such men is inferior to a nation run at higher pressure. The problem is, then, how can men be trained up to their most useful pitch of energy? And how can nations make such training most accessible to all their sons and daughters? This, after all, is only the general problem of education formulated in slightly different terms. . . .

FIVE Let no one think, then, that our problem of individual and national economy is solely that of the maximum of pounds raisable against gravity, the maximum of locomotion, or of agitation of any sort, that human beings can accomplish. That might signify little more than hurrying and jumping about in uncoordinated ways; whereas inner work, though it so often reinforces outer work, quite as often means its arrest. . . .

SIX The first point to agree upon in this enterprise is that *as a rule men habitually use only a small part of the powers which they actually possess and which they might use under appropriate conditions.*

SEVEN Everyone is familiar with the phenomenon of feeling more or less alive on different days. Everyone knows on any given day that there are energies slumbering in him which the incitements of that day do not call forth, but which he might display if these were greater. Most of us feel as if a sort of cloud weighed upon us, keeping us below our highest notch of clearness in disconcernment, sureness in reasoning, or firmness in deciding. Compared with what we ought to be, we are only half awake. Our fires are damped, our drafts are checked. We are making use of only a small part of our possible mental and physical resources. . . .

EIGHT Stating the thing broadly, the human individual thus lives usually far within his limits; he possesses powers of various sorts which he habitually fails to use. He energizes below his *maximum,* and he behaves below his *optimum.* . . . In every conceivable way, his life is contracted like the field of vision of an hysteric subject—but with less excuse, for the poor hysteric is diseased, while in the rest of us it is only an inveterate *habit*—the habit of inferiority to our full self—that is bad.

NINE   Admit so much, then, and admit also that the charge of being inferior to their full self is far truer of some men than of others; then the practical question ensues: *to what do the better men owe their escape? and, in the fluctuations which all men feel in their own degree of energizing, to what are the improvements due, when they occur?*

TEN   In general terms the answer is plain:

ELEVEN   Either some unusual stimulus fills them with emotional excitement, or some unusual idea of necessity induces them to make an extra effort of will. *Excitements, ideas, and efforts,* in a word, are what carry us over the dam.

TWELVE   In those "hyperesthetic" conditions which chronic invalidism so often brings in its train, the dam has changed its normal place. The slightest functional exercise gives a distress which the patient yields to and stops. In such cases of "habit-neurosis" a new range of power often comes in consequence of the "bullying-treatment," of efforts which the doctor obliges the patient, much against his will, to make. First comes the very extremity of distress, then follows unexpected relief. There seems no doubt that *we are each and all of us to some extent victims of habit-neurosis.* We have to admit the wider potential range and the habitually narrow actual use. We live subject to arrest by degrees of fatigue which we have come only from habit to obey. Most of us learn to push the barrier farther off, and to live in perfect comfort on much higher levels of power.

THIRTEEN   Country people and city people, as a class, illustrate this difference. The rapid rate of life, the number of decisions in an hour, the many things to keep account of, in a busy city man's or woman's life, seem monstrous to a country brother. He doesn't see how we live at all. A day in New York or Chicago fills him with terror. The danger and noise make it appear like a permanent earthquake. But *settle* him there, and in a year or two he will have caught the pulse beat. He will vibrate to the city's rhythms; and if he only succeeds in his avocation, whatever that may be, he will find a joy in all the hurry and the tension, he will keep the pace as well as any of us, and get as much out of himself in any week as he ever did in ten weeks in the country. . . .

FOURTEEN   The normal opener of deeper and deeper levels of energy is the will. The difficulty is to use it, to make the effort which the word volition implies. But if we *do* make it (or if a god, though he were only the god Chance, makes it through us), it will act dynamogenically on us for a month. It is notorious that a single successful effort of moral volition, such as saying "no" to some habitual temptation, or performing some courageous act, will launch a man on a higher level of energy for days and weeks, will give him a new range of power.

the energies of men

1. From the context, which of the following definitions is best for the word "efficacious"? (Par. 1: "That amount of fatigue is an *efficacious* obstruction on this side of which our usual life is cast.")
    a. maximum
    b. optimum
    c. effective
    d. relevant

2. What does William James say is the opener of deeper levels of energy in men?
    a. adrenalin
    b. society
    c. will
    d. habit

3. What is the purpose served by the figure of speech in which James claims "our fires are damped"? (Par. 7: "*Our fires are damped,* our drafts are checked.")
    a. it refers to our use of only a small part of our possible mental and physical resources
    b. it refers to the absence of God in many people
    c. it refers to the mental effects of life's disappointments and defeats
    d. it refers to the approach of death in a man

4. Which of the following best describes the pattern of development of this essay?
    a. a presentation and explanation of a phenomenon of life, with insight into the problems it creates, and how to overcome them
    b. a description of a fatigued person which emphasizes his inferiority
    c. a series of examples leading to the discovery of the phenomenon of second wind
    d. inductive reasoning about a phenomenon of life from some given examples

5. Which of the following words is used by James in an emotive sense?
    a. energizing (Par. 3: "His more active rate of *energizing* does not wreck him . . .")
    b. pitch (Par. 4: "How can men be trained up to their most useful *pitch* of energy?")
    c. volition (Par. 5: "The difficulty is to use it [will], to

make the effort which the word *volition* implies.")

d. weighed   (Par. 7: "Most of us feel as if a sort of cloud
                     weighed upon us . . .")

6. Which of the following best describes the tone of this essay?

   a. impersonal, formal presentation with an intent to be informative
   b. satirical with an underlying moral purpose
   c. argumentative with an underlying purpose to be con-
   vincingly informative to hostile readers
   d. impersonal with a dominant rhetorical purpose, the subject
   matter being of little concern to the author other than to be
   a mode of presenting his rhetorical form

7. Which of the following best describes the moral or philosophical attitude
   expressed in the essay?

   a. extreme distress is felt by one who tries to overcome habit-
   neurosis
   b. we are all victims of habit-neurosis and volition is the
   answer for freeing the deeper levels of energy in men
   c. our national government must assume federal control of
   education so that appropriate measures may be taken to
   motivate those who are inferior to their true selves
   d. fatigue is a disease of certain humans which we must be
   taught to recognize

8. Which of the following inferences seems most likely as a description of
   James' attitude toward those who have habit-neurosis?

   a. it is unnecessary for those people to live so near their surface because volition can give them a new range of power
   b. those people are mentally ill, and the distress they would
   feel from trying to overcome their illness would be too great
   c. those people would be looked upon with contempt, for they
   are lazy
   d. those people cannot help themselves, so we must feel sorry
   for them

9. What purpose is served by James's saying that "the trees don't grow into
   the sky"?

   a. stored up, unused energies stunt one's growth
   b. habitually we never push through the obstruction holding
   our energies back
   c. the phenomenon of second wind applies to plant life, as
   well as to men
   d. men have limits to their energies

10. Which of the following best describes the author's intention in the passage
    contrasting city people with country people?

    a. both city and country people energize below their maximum
    b. the innate abilities of country folk are probably inferior to
    those of city folk
    c. an environment of increased tension and pressure will help
    to launch a man to a higher level of energy
    d. the existence of rural areas causes our nation to be inferior

7

comments

The Memory Process

Some students do not try to develop better memories because they believe that one is "born with a good memory." We know, however, that memory can be developed by following sound principles of learning.

The following three steps are necessary to commit a specific idea to memory: first, one must thoroughly understand the idea so that a clear and accurate impression is gained; second, one must "embed" the idea in mind either by repeating it frequently or by using it over and over again; and third, one must intend to remember.

It is surprising how many students fail in the first step—to get an accurate impression of the idea from the beginning. This is especially true in the reading of textbooks. Most students plunge along the printed lines and seldom stop to ask, "What did the author say?" Without really knowing what the author said, one could hardly obtain a clear and accurate impression of the idea in the first place.

When these same students complain about forgetting, I am always tempted to say, "You cannot forget something you never had in the first place."

This first important step—getting an accurate impression—can be mastered simply by having a positive mental attitude. For example, the student who continually looks *for* something will be gathering accurate impressions more efficiently than the student who looks *at* something, whether it be words on a page, a painting, a person, or an incident. Bacon put this thought into focus on a larger scale when he said that the progress of science resulted not by staring at Nature, but by interrogating her.

Taking a cue thus from Bacon, a student can go far by asking questions of the author, then looking for answers, and thereby getting a clear understanding from the start.

In this selection, Professor Meenes brings a practical approach to the problem of memory from which every student should benefit.

The Memory Process

Max Meenes

The Nature of Memory

ONE   The memory process is apt to be misunderstood. Many believe that memory is a general ability which people possess in varying degrees. Thus some are said to have good memories, others poor ones. Many also are of the opinion that a weak memory, like a weak muscle, can be improved by exercise. Perhaps you have tried memorizing material solely for the sake of strengthening your memory. Psychologists have found that this cannot be done because there seems to be no memory-in-general. There are only specific memories. You may, by memorizing poetry, learn to memorize poetry more efficiently, but this will not help you to memorize the atomic weights of the chemical elements. Many recognize this fact when they say they have a good memory for faces but not for names or that they can remember names but not numbers. Memories are specific. This does not mean that you can do nothing about an inability to recall names or any other kind of material. You can acquire the necessary skill but it will, like any other acquisition, require practice. Practice may improve a specific kind of memory but you must not expect that exercising your memory for, say, poetry will improve your "memory-in-general." Often when a person complains of a poor memory for names, it turns out that what he should be saying is that he does not learn names easily. Much poor memory is really poor or inadequate learning. What you learn superficially or only part way you can hardly expect to remember. What you learn thoroughly is less likely to suffer forgetting.

Two   When the trouble originates in inadequate learning, the remedy is better learning. If you have difficulty remembering names, it is

Max Meenes, *Studying and Learning* (New York: Random House, Inc., 1954), by permission of Random House, Inc. Copyright 1954 by Random House, Inc.

first necessary that you hear the name distinctly. The name will need to be impressed by repetition; you will therefore use it often, perhaps writing it down. If you are interested in the person the name symbolizes, you will find it easier to remember his name. You can improve your memory for study material in the same way: see it accurately and clearly, practice it, value it.

THREE When you say you have a poor memory for something, you may be really saying you have no interest in it. Perhaps you cannot recall dates in history or the steps of chemical analysis. How well do you recall your school's football scores or who dated whom at the last prom? What you are interested in does seem easier to keep in memory. The effect of interest may be indirect; it impels you to study and repeat until you can recall. It may also be direct; dynamic factors like interest or need keep memory alive.

FOUR Memory is not a storage bin containing ideas intact and delivering them up as needed. What we learn is tied in with what we already know. It is recalled when the correct cue or stimulus appears. But during the process of assimilation, ideas may become altered to fit the larger pattern which absorbs them. Memories may be modified to fit our frame of reference. They may change to conform to our needs. Thus the two-pound fish we caught grows in weight with each recall. What is recalled is not a simple reproduction of what has been learned. Memory is fluid.

FIVE Another erroneous idea that is often entertained is that the slow learner has a better memory than the rapid learner. The evidence from carefully controlled experiments points in the opposite direction. When slow and fast learners are permitted to learn the same material to the same degree, the rapid learners retain more than slow ones. Of course, if the slow student overlearns, he will retain more than the rapid learner who is content with less practice. Since rapid learning is associated with good memory, you may expect better recall as you improve your learning efficiency.

Time and Forgetting

SIX When nonsense syllables are learned to the point where the subject is just capable of reproducing them correctly, about half will be forgotten within twenty minutes. Forgetting continues after that, of course, but at a slower rate. The greatest amount of forgetting occurs within a short time after the original learning. Meaningful material, while forgotten less rapidly than meaningless, also suffers its greatest loss shortly after it has been learned. If material is very greatly overlearned it may not be forgotten at all. The skills we acquire are usually practiced so much after being learned that they may never be forgotten. Verbal material that is practiced a great deal may also be retained indefinitely. But it is not usually practicable for the student to overlearn his assignment so thoroughly. Relearning, as shown earlier, is more efficient than overlearning.

SEVEN It might be supposed, from the fact that such a high proportion is forgotten in a short period directly after learning, that relearning should preferably occur about half an hour after the first learning. This would keep the student relearning every half-hour. There is, however, no evidence that relearning every half-hour will bring about better retention than relearning every day, or even at greater intervals.

EIGHT Not all parts of the material learned are forgotten to the same degree. The first and last portions of a poem or a lesson are retained much better than the middle portion. This again is an instance where easier learning makes for better retention, for the first and last parts are learned long before the middle. It follows from this that the middle portion should not only receive extra stress in learning, but should also get special attention in relearning.

Interference and Forgetting

NINE Some psychologists emphasize the effect of disuse on forgetting. For them the longer the period of time without use, the greater the forgetting. Every time learning is used it is strengthened and therefore better retained. This is demonstrated in a variety of experiments involving especially the conditioned-response kind of learning.

TEN Other psychologists believe that forgetting is not a matter of use and disuse but rather the effect of interference from other learning. What we learn is forgotten, according to them, because other things learned block the recall. This inhibition can come from two directions. Earlier learning may interfere with the memory of later learning or later learning may inhibit the recall of the earlier. The former is proactive inhibition, and the latter retroactive inhibition.

ELEVEN There is always the possibility of interference among learned materials. What has been learned earlier may reduce the memory for what is to be learned later. If two poems are learned one after the other, the learning of the first one reduces the ability to recall the second one. This is only part of the story. Retroactive inhibition also takes place; the second poem interferes with the recall of the first. Thus there is some interference from both directions. The amount of interference among learned items is, however, not usually a serious problem for the learner. The amount of interference is greatest in the early stages of learning. The better the degree of learning, the less the amount of interference. The remedy for inhibition is more complete learning. Another fact about this interference is that it diminishes with time. This is another reason why short frequent study periods are more efficient than a long single period. In short periods there is less accumulation of inhibition and the amount that does accumulate diminishes between study periods.

TWELVE Inhibition is affected by similarity. If two similar things are learned, the inhibitory effect of the second on the recall of the first is greater than if dissimilar items are studied. For this reason it is desirable to arrange your study periods so as to separate the study of similar subjects. If you are taking English, French, and psychology, inhibition will be less if you study your subjects in the order: English, psychology, French. The two languages are more alike than either language and psychology; therefore they should not be studied one right after the other.

THIRTEEN Inhibitory effects show up in the form of confusion and error as well as failure to recall. These confusions are especially likely to occur among learned items that are similar. It is easier to make the mistake of calling "Fitzpatrick" "Fitzgerald" than to confuse either name with "Jones." Since the first part of the two names is identical, "Fitz" serves as a cue to both "gerald" and "patrick." 'Smith," on the other hand, might be confused with "Jones" because they are both associated with commonness of name. Thus similarity may produce interference rather than facilitation in learning. To avoid this kind of confusion, it is important to note with care resemblances and differences when studying. Noting resemblances adds meaning to the learning but may produce trouble in memory. Observing differences will prevent confusion in recall.

the memory process

1. From the context which of the following definitions is best for the word, inhibition? (Par. 2: "The remedy for *inhibition* is more complete learning.")
   a. frustration
   b. interference
   c. restraint
   d. prohibition

2. The greatest amount of forgetting occurs:
   a. when the material is overlearned
   b. in a short time after the original learning
   c. with nonsense syllables
   d. after relearning takes place

3. What purpose is served by referring to memory as "*not* being a storage bin"?
   a. it implies that memory does not conform to our needs and is not a receptacle for all ideas
   b. it is not possible to keep ideas intact and stored in a convenient spot

     c. it tries to show that ideas are not kept intact and delivered up as needed
     d. it suggests that we tend to recall things as we would like them to be

4. Which of the following phrases best describes the pattern of development of this article?
     a. an example followed by a comment on it
     b. a generality followed by describing its parts
     c. examples followed by a moral insight based on the examples
     d. a statement followed by an explanation

5. Which of the following words is used in an emotive sense?
     a. inadequate   (Par. 1: "Much poor memory is really poor or *inadequate* learning.")
     b. dynamic   (Par. 3: "It may also be dynamic; *dynamic* factors like interest or need keep memory alive.")
     c. inhibition   (Par. 12: "*Inhibition* is affected by similarity.")
     d. weak   (Par. 1: "Many also are of the opinion that a weak memory, like a *weak* muscle, can be improved by exercise.")

6. Which of the following best describes the tone of this article?
     a. satirical and impersonal
     b. rhetorical and impersonal
     c. descriptive and moralistic
     d. logical and impersonal

7. Which of the following best describes the psychological attitude expressed in the first part of the article titled, "The Nature of Memory"?
     a. memory is an ability people posess in varying degrees
     b. a weak memory may be improved by the proper exercise
     c. a slow learner has a better memory than a rapid learner
     d. a specific kind of memory may be improved through practice

8. Which of the following inferences seems most likely in the author's explanation of "Interference and Forgetting"?
     a. that learning is affected by inhibitions of various kinds
     b. that forgetting takes place when knowledge is not used
     c. that learning is facilitated by short study periods
     d. that observing differences in learning material rather than similarities will help recall

9. What purpose is served by the author's showing that Fitzpatrick may be confused with Fitzgerald but not Jones?
     a. to show that Jones is such a common name that it is not easily confused with other names
     b. to show that interest in a person and his name will make it easier to remember
     c. to show that retroactive inhibition is taking place
     d. to show that similarities may produce interference rather than ease in learning

10. Which of the following best describes the author's intention in this article?

 a. that memory can be improved if specific things are kept in mind concerning the memory process

 b. that memory is fluid, that ideas cannot be stored intact and delivered up when needed

 c. that the first and last thing you learn is remembered much better than the middle part

 d. that forgetting is the effect of interference from other learning

part iv

On Ethics

One may rightfully wonder why the topic of *ethics* was included in a book of this sort. The answer is that effective and efficient learning depends, to a great degree, on healthy attitudes.

The sooner a student thinks through his relationship to the world at large, the sooner will he be equipped mentally, emotionally, and ethically to become a scholar.

The first selection deals with the ancient topic best described by these words, ". . . if thine enemy hunger, feed him; if he thirst, give him drink . . ."

Think not that hatred is expelled from the breasts of educated men who dwell in ivory towers, for it is as common there as in the breasts of those who slink in the dark alleys of our cities

The second selection on *plagarism* stresses the ethical responsibility of the student to the intellectual community. He is urged to strengthen, not weaken, the integrity of the strong chain of scholarship which has been wrought link by link by generations of men from Homer to the present.

It is well to ponder the questions raised by these

two selections and the solutions suggested. When similar problems confront you, as they surely will, you will have at least some stored-up wisdom to stem the initial onslaught of temptation, which, too, will surely come.

8

comments

The Futility of Hate

In this selection the president of Yale University, in his sermon to the graduating seniors, deliberately chose a topic which he felt the students would need most and would do the most lasting good.

I believe that President Griswold had seen the withering effects of hate on people of various stations: the educated as well as the uneducated who have thrown away happiness and delight, family and friend, because of "wanting to get even" with someone.

Stop to think about the concept of hate! What an ambition to have: "I'm going to get even with that guy if its the last thing I do!" Life is hard enough for everyone—the hated as well as the hater—without someone deliberately determined to make life even harder for some soul.

Though the ethical principle, "overcome evil with good" has come down in the distilled wisdom of the ages, still the pages of history show that the principle has not been taken to heart by all. Therefore, a second line of defense is brought into the attack: When you hate, you destroy yourself, not the object of your hate.

This—that hate is an inevitable boomerang; that hate is the act of self-poisoning—has helped more people to follow the ethical commandment than the words of the commandment itself.

Go, therefore, and hate no more, ever.

The Futility of Hate

Alfred Whitney Griswold

Recompense to no man evil for evil.
    . . . if thine enemy hunger, feed him; if he thirst, give him
    drink . . .
Be not overcome of evil, but overcome evil with good.
                                            ROMANS 12:17, 20, 21

ONE Suppose St. Paul had just written these words in an Epistle to the Americans. How would they be received? If we thought of our enemies as the Russians and the Chinese the chances are we might reject the Apostle's advice as visionary or, still worse, appeasement. If we thought of enemies nearer home, enemies of the republic real or imagined, or personal enemies of any sort our feelings might be much the same. In either case our first impulse would probably be to throw up our hands and say, How can we be kind to our enemies when they won't let us? How can we penetrate the Iron Curtain? How can we reach the heart or conscience of those who would overthrow the government by conspiracy and violence or who, in more intimate circumstances, seek our own undoing?

TWO There is no easy answer to these questions. Certainly appeasement is not one. In the tarnished meaning it has acquired in recent usage, appeasement means offering your watch to the hold-up man in the hope of persuading him not to take your pocketbook. It has become synonymous with bribery and blackmail. St. Paul was counseling magnanimity and charity, qualities that spring from courage, not fear; from strength, not weakness. As we have learned to our sorrow, appeasement produces contempt and further aggression rather than gratitude, justice, and peace. This is true whether we apply it to international, national, or personal affairs. It is as far a cry from what St. Paul was talking about as it is from practical policy for our own times.

THREE But if appeasing our enemies is not an answer, neither is hating them. History shows us nothing more clearly than the sheer sterility of hate. Again and again, in life and in the great literary classics it has inspired, we see hate destroying the hater, not the hated, as it

Alfred Whitney Griswold, *In the University Tradition.* Baccalaureate sermon to the graduating class, June 12, 1955. Reprinted by permission of Yale University Press.

destroyed Saul in his enmity for David, Ahab in his pursuit of Moby Dick, and Adolf Hitler in his bunker in Berlin. Though there may be no obvious or easy way of winning over our enemies through kindness, hating them is an alternative far less likely to deter them than it is to hurt us. Somewhere between the extremes of appeasement and hate there is a place for courage and strength to express themselves in magnanimity and charity. This is the place we must find if we are to be true to the basic tenents of our Christian faith as well as to ourselves as Americans and as citizens of the world. This is St. Paul's message to the Romans and through the Romans to us who have fallen heir to their civilization.

Four   Of the two extremes, hate and appeasement, hate is the more difficult to avoid. The times have taught us the folly of appeasement. But they have never yet quite taught us the folly of hate. What is this mysterious passion that gulls mankind? In the abstract it can be pure and noble, as it is, for example, when applied to evil, when we hate cruelty, injustice, and oppression. But when hate seeks out concrete embodiments of these and other detestable qualities and concentrates on them, it becomes corrupt. Or rather, it becomes corrupting. For now, no matter what the circumstances—the nature of the evil, the degree of provocation, the sense of outrage—hate begins to inject its subtle poisons into the hater; and unless the process is promptly checked, it is he who will suffer, not the person or thing he hates.

Five   There are, it is true, instances of reciprocity in which both parties suffer equally, as do the Montague and Capulet families in the death of Romeo and Juliet. Sometimes the hater seems to accomplish his objectives only to find himself ruined in the bargain, like Iago in *Othello*. More often than not the hater is consumed by his own fury while the world passes him by and the object of his passion remains untouched. He makes a fool of himself—not merely an object of ridicule, but the author and victim of tragic mistakes. He becomes a bore and misanthrope, forfeiting the sympathy of his friends, accomplishing nothing save the shrinking of his own soul.

Six   This may be why Dickens depicts hate in the figure of a dwarf, the odious Daniel Quilp of *The Old Curiosity Shop*. Quilp is a usurer, whose trade Dickens was at pains to disparage, but he is also the pure embodiment of hate. He hates his wife, his friends, his business associates. He makes wax images of his victims and melts them. One of the most malevolent and revolting of all Dickens' characters, he comes to his end with the law at his heels by falling into the Thames in a frenzy of rage and drowning. The point does not lie in the plot so much as it does in the fact that when Dickens, with his matchless insight into human nature, sought to represent hate, he did so in a form so stunted and loathesome.

Seven   Perhaps the most awe-inspiring of all such representations of hate is Ahab, Captain of the *Pequod*, in Melville's classic *Moby Dick*.

Through this long, brooding narrative Ahab drives himself, his ship, and his crew in vengeful pursuit of the white whale to which he has already lost a leg and now loses his soul. He had conceived, says Melville, "a wild vindictiveness against the whale. . . . He piled upon the whale's white hump the sum of all the general rage and hate felt by his whole race from Adam down."

EIGHT   Thus the foundations of the tragedy are laid. The secret of his rage pent up within him, Ahab prepares for the voyage with the sole purpose of hunting Moby Dick. Had the *Pequod's* owners and their associates suspected this they would quickly have taken the ship away from him. For, as Melville reminds us, their aim was a profitable cruise, while Ahab was intent on personal revenge. His very crew seemed chosen for his purpose, ranging as it did from castaways and cannibals to right-minded but weak-willed officers. When the test came they bent to his will as their ship did to the gales of the Pacific. They became infected by his hate even though they neither shared his motives nor understood his objectives. It is evident from the outset that hate has bereft Ahab of his competence, and that all who surround him will suffer from his warped judgment and mistaken methods as well as from the contagion of his hate.

NINE   All attempts to reason with Ahab fail before his obsession. Repeatedly Starbuck, the *Pequod's* mate, with wife and infant son in Nantucket, implores him to abandon his quest only to be dismissed with ravings about some hidden master that "against all natural lovings and longings" drives him on. When the whale is at last sighted and the chase begun, Starbuck redoubles his pleadings, but in vain. Three times Ahab lowers his boats only to have them smashed in wild encounters with the free-swimming whale. "Great God but for one single instant show thy-self," cries Starbuck at the end of the second day, "never never wilt thou capture him, old man—Two days chased; twice stove to splinters; thy very leg once more snatched from under thee;—all good angels mobing these with warnings—what more would'st thou have?" But the captain has turned over his command to the hater and the hater to the madman. "Fool!" he replies. "I am the Fates' lieutenant; I act under orders." Right up to the last, Starbuck pleads, "See! Moby Dick seeks thee not. It is thou, thou, that madly seekest him!" But Ahab will not desist until the goaded whale has killed him, then turned on the *Pequod* itself and sent the ship with all its boats and their crews to the bottom. No one who has read *Moby Dick* will forget the desolation of that scene from which only Ishmael miraculously escapes to recount this epic of hate.

TEN   Of the living embodiments of hate to which our own times have been witness, the classic is Hitler. So fresh and indelible is his baleful image that I need not enlarge upon it here. No ordinary impulse motivated Hitler. Here was hate sublimated and exalted into a doctrine, an ethic, a way of life. Yet its end was the same as that of the tragicomic dwarf of Dickens' novel and the demoniac whaling captain of *Moby Dick*. It brought suffering and destruction to millions of human souls. But it failed to accomplish its objectives, and it destroyed its progenitor.

ELEVEN   There is still another aspect of hate to which our times are witness and to which the counsel of St. Paul is relevant. This is the doctrine of hate derived from Karl Marx. It springs, in its origin, not only from an objective sense of injustice, but from subjective unhappiness and misanthropy. Whatever its origin, the very fact that it is compounded of hate exposes it to the ultimate fate of Quilp and Ahab and Hitler. Whatever we may think of it, to answer those who preach it in kind exposes us to the same fate.

TWELVE   St. Paul, no less than the present leaders of communism, was trying to build the foundations of a new world order. But St. Paul's foundations were those of Christ, who believed that compassion and love were elemental, universal, and omnipresent in the human race; that they were not only the most noble instincts in man but the most powerful and constructive; and that they would unfailingly serve the best interests of man whenever, and in whatever circumstances he would make use of them. Is this so hard for us to believe? The structure resting upon these foundations has lasted nearly two thousand years, offering comfort and hope to all mankind, providing them to millions in many nations. The structure erected upon the foundations of Marx is not yet forty years old. How many men it truly shelters is impossible to say, for it is maintained by tyranny and veiled in secrecy. But which of the two is the house built upon rock and which the house built upon sand we can tell by looking at their respective foundations.

THIRTEEN   Gentlemen of the senior class: life offers you a choice in these matters. It offers you also certain guarantees based upon human experience. The examples I have cited to you this morning suggest the worth of these guarantees in shaping your own affairs and the affairs of your country. But the choice is yours. You must have courage and strength to make it, otherwise it will not be a free choice; and an unfree choice is as good as none. To a free man as to a free country, and to a strong man as to a strong country, the wisdom of St. Paul commends itself as the only alternative. Let us hope for ourselves and for our country that courage and strength may guide us to this wisdom and so lead us on to new strength and courage.

the futility of hate

1.   From the context, which of the following definitions is best for the word, *sterility*? (Par. 3: "History shows us nothing more clearly than the sheer *sterility* of hate.")

     a. barrenness

        b. unprofitableness
        c. impotence
        d. unfruitfulness

2. Quilp is a character in:
        a. Moby Dick
        b. Othello
        c. The Old Curiosity Shop
        d. Mein Kampf

3. What is the purpose of the figure of speech, "hate begins to inject its subtle poisons into the hater?"
        a. to illustrate how this "mysterious passion gulls mankind"
        b. to explain what happens when "hate seeks out concrete embodiments" of cruelty, injustice, and oppression
        c. to dramatize hate, the corrupter
        d. to emphasize that "hate [destroys] the hater, not the hated"

4. Which of the following phrases best describes the pattern of development of this passage?
        a. from a hypothetical situation to the actual situation confronting the senior class
        b. drawing on literary allusions and texts to support a point of view
        c. illustrating and defining extremes in search of a middle road
        d. a contrast between two alternatives, appeasement and hate

5. Which of the following words is used by the author in an emotive sense?

        a. desolation   (Par. 9: "No one who has read *Moby Dick* will forget the *desolation* of that scene. . . .")

        b. bereft   (Par. 8: "It is evident from the outset that hate has *bereft* Ahab of his competence. . . .")

        c. indelible   (Par. 10: "So fresh and *indelible* is his baleful image that I need not enlarge upon it here.")

        d. appeasement   (Par. 1: ". . . we might reject the Apostle's advice as visionary or, still worse, *appeasement.*")

6. Which of the following best describes the tone of this passage?
        a. descriptive and philosophical
        b. personal and definitive
        c. moral and optimistic
        d. all of these

7. Which of the following best describes the moral or philosophical attitude expressed in the concluding paragraph?
        a. each individual must choose for himself
        b. one can confidently base his choice on his knowledge of human experience
        c. an unfree choice is as good as none
        d. the wisdom of St. Paul is the only foundation for free men and a free country

8. Which of the following inferences seems most likely as a description of the author's intent in speaking about "the house built upon rock," and "the house built upon sand"? (Par. 12)

    a. we can determine which house is built upon rock and which upon sand

    b. the structure with the firmest foundation is inevitably superior

    c. St. Paul's world order is "built upon rock," Marx's "upon sand"

    d. compassion and love are a firmer foundation than tyranny and secrecy

9. What purpose is served by the various literary allusions?

    a. to illustrate "concrete embodiments" of hate

    b. to prove that hate destroys the hater not the hated

    c. to teach the folly of hate

    d. to underscore the futility of hate

10. Which of the following best describes the author's intention in this passage?

    a. to seek an alternative to appeasement

    b. to exhort Americans and all peoples to "overcome evil with good"

    c. to convince the graduating class of the correct choice

    d. to urge an end to the "cold war"

9

comments

A Definition of Plagiarism

The author plainly equates plagiarism with embezzlement. He argues his case in terms of intellectual and moral honesty. I agree that there is no better argument against plagiarism; but what bothers me is that plagiarism still continues.

There is no question in my mind regarding the basic honesty of college students in general, but when a normally honest student is placed in a situation of intense pressure, then a type of fear often beclouds his judgment, and I am afraid that he, at the moment, thinks not with his "ethical" mind, but with his "emotive" mind. Since this is often the case, perhaps a more persuasive means should be presented to deter students from using as their own someone else's words and thoughts. I suggest that students vizualize the consequences.

Since it is practically impossible to get away with plagiarism, the plagiarist will be discovered, confronted, accused, and usually dismissed from the university. The act once done cannot be undone—cannot be erased from the blackboards of mind and conscience. Years hence the student-plagiarist may writhe in his sleep, wake up in a cold sweat, and hope that the original act was a dream which would vanish with awakening; but alas! the scene is etched, fixed, and indelible. He cannot wipe it, nor claw it out of existence.

Remember, no matter where you find the tempting passage, either in a much used reference book or a dust covered tome in some dark recess of the library's attic, someone, too, had read it before. Remember, your professor was a graduate student once, he researched and pored over everything he could lay his hands on: he has read hundreds—nay, thousands—of papers of past classes; he knows the ideas and words of almost all who have written on the subject. Furthermore, a smooth sentence or a smooth thought injected in the midst of a student's tortured phraseology shouts out, "I've been kidnapped!" as the professor's eyes glide over it.

Though I'm not well versed in Ezra Pound's writing, yet I believe that I could identify some of his thoughts and style in a student's paper. Take this group of words: ". . . or that are likely to be frequently needed for reference." Read this group of words aloud; notice how smooth and decidedly rhythmic the words are, especially, the portion, "likely to be frequently."

My advice is, don't do it, you'll be caught; then, all the tears in the world won't wash out the stain which will permeate your reputation.

Instead, put quotations around that which you feel cannot be said better; the rest of the references and data should be processed through your mind until you can hurl forth words to express them. The words may not be great, but they are your words, and even then footnote the origin of the new data.

The most tempting type of plagiarism—a type which the freshmen believes no one ever thought of, or that no professor would be able to disentangle—is the "mosaic." But, notice how well it is known. Notice how well the author has identified it and expounded on it. All the techniques are known.

The distilled essence of the ages—the ages which have seen all manner of suffering—shouts out, "Thou shalt not steal."

A Definition of Plagiarism

Harold C. Martin and Richard M. Ohmann

ONE The academic counterpart of the bank embezzler and of the manufacturer who mislabels his product is the plagiarist, the student or scholar who leads his reader to believe that what he is reading is the original work of the writer when it is not. If it could be assumed that the distinction between plagiarism and honest use of sources is perfectly clear in everyone's mind, there would be no need for the explanation that follows; merely the warning with which this definition concludes would be enough. But it is apparent that sometimes men of good will draw the suspicion of guilt upon themselves (and, indeed, are guilty) simply because they are not aware of the illegitimacy of certain kinds of "borrowing" and of the procedures for correct identification of materials other than those gained through independent research and reflection.

Two The spectrum is a wide one. At one end there is word-for-word copying of another's writing without enclosing the copied passage in quotation marks and identifying it in a footnote, *both* of which are necessary. (This includes, of course, the copying of all or any part of another student's paper.) It hardly seems possible that anyone of college age or more could do that without clear intent to deceive. At the other end there is the almost casual slipping in of a particularly apt term which one has come across in reading and which so admirably expresses one's opinion that one is tempted to make it personal property. Between these poles there are degrees and degrees, but they may be roughly placed in two groups. Close to outright and blatant deceit—but more the result, perhaps, of laziness than of bad intent—is the patching together of random jottings made in the course of reading, generally without careful identification of their source, and then woven into the text, so that the result is a mosaic of other people's ideas and words, the writer's sole contribution being the cement to hold the pieces together. Indicative of more effort and, for that reason, somewhat closer to honesty, though still dishonest, is the paraphrase, an abbreviated (and often skillfully prepared) restatement of someone else's analysis or conclusion without acknowledgement that another person's text has been the basis for the recapitulation.

Three The examples given below should make clear the dishonest and the proper use of source material. If instances occur which these examples do not seem to cover, conscience will in all likelihood be prepared to supply advice.

The Source

Four The importance of the *Second Treatise of Government* printed in this volume is such that without it we should miss some of the familiar features of our own government. It is safe to assert that the much criticized branch known as the Supreme Court obtained its being as a result of Locke's insistence upon the separation of powers; and that the combination of many powers in the hands of the executive under the New Deal has still to encounter opposition because it is contrary to the principles enunciated therein, the effect of which is not spent, though the relationship may not be consciously traced. Again we see the crystallizing force of Locke's writing. It renders explicit and adapts to the British politics of his day the trend and aim of writers from Languet and Bodin through Hooker and Grotius, to say nothing of the distant ancients, Aristotle and the Stoic school of natural law. It sums up magistrally the arguments used through the ages to attack authority vested in a single individual, but it does so from the particular point of view engendered by the Revolution of 1688 and is in harmony with the British scene and mental climate of the growing bourgeoisie of that age. Montesquieu and Rousseau, the framers of our own Declaration of Independence, and the statesmen (or should we say merchants and speculators?) who drew up the Constitution have re-echoed its claims for human liberty, for the separation of powers, for the sanctity of private property. In the hands of these it has been the quarry of liberal doctrines; and that it has served the Socialist theory of property based on labor is final proof of its breadth of view.

> Charles L. Sherman, "Introduction" to John Locke, *Treatise of Civil Government* and *A Letter Concerning Toleration.*

1. *Word-For-Word Plagiarizing*

FIVE It is not hard to see the importance of the *Second Treatise of Government* to our own democracy. Without it we should miss some of the most familiar features of our own government. It is safe to assert that the much criticized branch known as the Supreme Court obtained its being as a result of Locke's insistence upon the separation of powers; and that the combination of many powers in the hands of the executive under the New Deal has still to encounter opposition because it is contrary to the principles enunciated therein, the effect of which is not spent, though the relationship may not be consciously traced. The framers of our own Declaration of Independence and the statesmen who drew up the Constitution have re-echoed its claims for human liberty, for the separation of powers, for the sanctity of private property. All these are marks of the influence of Locke's *Second Treatise* on our own way of life.

SIX In this example, after composing half of a first sentence, the writer copies exactly what is in the original text, leaving out the center section of the paragraph and omitting the names of Montesquieu and Rousseau where he takes up the text again. The last sentence is also the writer's own.

SEVEN If the writer had enclosed all the copied text in quotation marks and had identified the source in a footnote, he would not have been liable to the charge of plagiarism; a reader might justifiably have felt, however, that the writer's personal contribution to the discussion was not very significant.

2. *The Mosaic*

EIGHT   The crystallizing force of Locke's writing may be seen in the effect his *Second Treatise of Government* had in shaping some of the familiar features of our own government. That much criticized branch known as the Supreme Court and the combination of many powers in the hands of the executive under the New Deal are modern examples. But even the foundations of our state—the Declaration of Independence and the Constitution—have re-echoed its claims for human liberty, for the separation of powers, for the sanctity of private property. True, the influence of others is also marked in our Constitution—from the trend and aim of writers like Languet and Bodin, Hooker and Grotius, to say nothing of Aristotle and the Stoic school of natural law; but the fundamental influence is Locke's *Treatise*, the very quarry of liberal doctrines.

NINE   Note how the following phrases have been lifted out of the original text and moved into new patterns:

crystallizing force of Locke's writing
some of the familiar features of our own government
much criticized branch known as the Supreme Court
combination of many powers in the hands of the executive under the New Deal
have re-echoed its claims for human liberty . . . property
from the trend and aim . . . Grotius
to say nothing of Aristotle and . . . natural law
quarry of liberal doctrines

TEN   As in the first example, there is really no way of legitimizing such a procedure. To put every stolen phrase within quotation marks would produce an almost unreadable, and quite worthless, text.

3. *The Paraphrase*

ELEVEN

PARAPHRASE: Many fundamental aspects of our own government are
ORIGINAL: Many familiar features of our own government are

apparent in the *Second Treatise of Government*. One can safely
apparent in the *Second Treatise of Government*. It is safe to

say that the oft-censured Supreme Court really owes its exis-
assert that the much criticized . . . Court obtained its being as

tence to the Lockeian demand that powers in government be kept
a result of Locke's insistence upon the separation of powers;

separate; equally one can say that the allocation of varied
and that the combination of many powers

and widespread authority to the President during the era of
in the hands of the executive under the

the New Deal has still to encounter opposition because it is
New Deal has still to encounter opposition because it is

contrary to the principles enunciated therein . . . . Once more it
contrary to the principles enunciated therein . . . . Again we see

is possible to note the way in which Locke's writing clarified
the crystallizing force of Locke's writing

existing opinion.

TWELVE   The foregoing interlinear presentation shows clearly how
the writer has simply traveled along with the original text, substituting
approximately equivalent terms except where his understanding fails
him, as it does with "crystallizing," or where the ambiguity of the original
is too great a tax on his ingenuity for him to proceed, as it is with "to
encounter opposition . . . consciously traced" in the original.

THIRTEEN   Such a procedure as the one shown in this example has
its uses; for one thing it is valuable for the student's own understanding
of the passage; and it may be valuable for the reader as well. How, then,
may it be properly used? The procedure is simple. The writer might
begin the second sentence with: "As Sherman notes in the introduction
to his edition of the *Treatise,* one can safely say . . ." and conclude the
paraphrased passage with a footnote giving the additional identification
necessary. Or he might indicate directly the exact nature of what he is
doing, in this fashion: "To paraphrase Sherman's comment . . ." and
conclude that also with a footnote indicator.

FOURTEEN   In point of fact, the source here used does not particularly lend itself to honest paraphrase, with the exception of that one
sentence which the paraphraser above copied without change except for
abridgement. The purpose of paraphrase should be to simplify or to
throw a new and significant light on a text; it requires much skill if it is
to be honestly used and should rarely be resorted to by the student
except for the purpose, as was suggested above, of his personal en-
lightenment.

4. The "Apt" Term

FIFTEEN   The *Second Treatise of Government* is a veritable
quarry of liberal doctrines. In it the crystallizing force of Locke's
writing is markedly apparent. The cause of human liberty, the
principle of separation of powers, and the inviolability of private
property—all three, major dogmas of American constitutionalism—

owe their presence in our Constitution in large part to the remarkable *Treatise* which first appeared around 1685 and was destined to spark, within three years, a revolution in the land of its author's birth and, ninety years later, another revolution against that land.

SIXTEEN   Here the writer has not been able to resist the appropriation of two striking terms—"quarry of liberal doctrines" and "crystallizing force"; a perfectly proper use of the terms would have required only the addition of a phrase: *The Second Treatise of Government* is, to use Sherman's suggestive expression, a "quarry of liberal doctrines." In it the "crystallizing force"—the term again is Sherman's—of Locke's writing is markedly apparent. . . .

SEVENTEEN   Other phrases in the text above—"the cause of human liberty," "the principle of the separation of powers," "the inviolability of private property"—are clearly drawn directly from the original source but are so much matters in the public domain, so to speak, that no one could reasonably object to their re-use in this fashion.

EIGHTEEN   Since one of the principal aims of a college education is the development of intellectual honesty, it is obvious that plagiarism is a particularly serious offense and the punishment for it is commensurately severe. What a penalized student suffers can never really be known by anyone but himself; what the student who plagiarizes and "gets away with it" suffers is less public and probably less acute, but the corruptness of his act, the disloyalty and baseness it entails, must inevitably leave a mark on him as well as on the institution of which he is a member.

a definition of plagiarism

1. From the context, which of the following definitions is best for the word, *crystallizing?* (Par. 8: "The *crystallizing* force of Locke's writing may be seen in the effect his *Second Treatise of Government* had in shaping some of the familiar features of our own government.")

   a. clarifying
   b. causing to assume a fixed and definite form
   c. transparent
   d. solidifying

2. According to the author, which type of plagiarism "has its uses; is valuable for the student's understanding of a passage"?

   a. mosaic
   b. apt term
   c. word-for-word
   d. paraphrase

3. What purpose is served by referring to a particular kind of plagiarism as a mosaic?
     a. art forms are deceiving
     b. a mosaic is a patchwork of materials
     c. the process of weaving other people's words and ideas into a text is similar to the process of making a mosaic
     d. all mosaics are randomly put together

4. Which of the following phrases best describes the pattern of development of this passage?
     a. definition and warning
     b. analogies and examples
     c. description of the spectrum of plagiarism
     d. definition and explanation through examples with a statement of the moral issue in the conclusion

5. Which of the following words is used by the author in an emotive sense?
     a. blatant   (Par. 2: "Close to outright and blatant deceit . . . is the patching . . .")
     b. conscience   (Par. 3: ". . . *conscience* will in all likelihood be prepared to supply.")
     c. stolen phrase (Par. 10: "To put every *stolen phrase* within quotation marks . . .")
     d. corruptness (Par. 18: ". . . but the *corruptness* of his act, the disloyalty and baseness it entails . . .")

6. Which of the following best describes the tone of this passage?
     a. descriptive and moralistic
     b. emotive and serious
     c. impersonal and descriptive
     d. moralistic and cynical

7. Which of the following best describes the moral or philosophical attitude expressed in the conclusion?
     a. the student who is penalized for plagiarism suffers more than the student who plagiarizes and "gets away with it"
     b. plagiarism is a corrupt, disloyal, base act
     c. a student should refrain from plagiarism because the act leaves an ineradicable mark on him and his school
     d. plagiarism is antithetical to one of the principal aims of a college education, the development of intellectual honesty

8. Which of the following inferences seems most likely as a description of the author's attitude toward paraphrasing when he says in Paragraph 13: "Such a procedure . . . has its uses; it is valuable for the student's own understanding of the passage . . . and it may be valuable for the reader as well. How, then, may it properly be used?"
     a. paraphrasing is a justifiable form of plagiarism
     b. because paraphrasing is valuable for the student's understanding and for the reader as well, it is permissible
     c. paraphrasing properly used can simplify or throw a significant light on the text
     d. paraphrasing is proper if credit is given in both text and footnote

9. What is the purpose of including a source and examples?
  a. to illustrate the spectrum of plagiarism
  b. to compare different types of plagiarism
  c. to make clear the dishonest and the proper use of source materials
  d. to show different interpretations of one source

10. Which of the following best describes the author's intention in this passage?
  a. to define plagiarism
  b. to point out the moral issue involved in plagiarism
  c. to explain a distinction which he feels is not perfectly clear in everyone's mind
  d. to chastise plagiarists

part v

On Writing

At best, writing is a difficult job, but an extremely gratifying one when done well. As a student, you will have to write sketches and "long papers" for English, and research papers and reports for almost all your other subjects; whether you like it or not, you will have to do a great deal of writing during your years in college.

It is terribly discouraging to a senior to find himself still struggling with the same trial-and-error method that he used when a freshman. He still stares at the blank sheet and tries to "tune in" on the right wave length, while hoping that a verbal stream—a hundred feet long—will be attracted to the antenna of his pen and flow through the nib onto the paper correctly, sagely, beautifully.

But wait! The pen moves; it scratches faster and faster; but, lo! it slows, slows, jerks, then stops abruptly and finally. He pauses to read the magic line, then wads up the paper and hurls it without glee to cluster with an already white heap of discarded attempts both in and around the basket.

But the paper is due tomorrow! He pulls himself together for another onslaught, and the cycle begins again. 'Tis sad to see. Somewhere along the line, this random writing has to stop and systematic improvement must begin. There is no surer way to place yourself on the right path than by writing; but now, always writing with certain sound principles in mind. The path will be rough, but remember, you will be improving with each step—and from each year's place of pausing your perspective will be increasingly clear and broad. The next two papers will help you to begin your uphill journey.

10

comments

Criteria for Good Writing

In the following selection, Professor Hathaway offers a fresh approach to all students who want to learn to express themselves more effectively. Professor Hathaway states his approach as follows:

> . . . The philosophy of the approach has been to emphasize constructive elements: to assist the student to establish new and better writing habits rather than to concentrate upon the analysis of common faults. This of course does not mean that faults are ignored, for recognition of the qualities of good writing is impossible without recognition of the ways in which good writing differs from bad. The stress here is placed upon the fundamentals of clear sentence structure and the effective organization of sentences in larger units. . . .
>
> Because the writer can be easily led—and too often is led—to worry about what not to do, we need an approach to the study of language that is positive; thus as his studies progress, the writer can add to his habits and techniques and not merely subtract from them. He needs to increase his range, not restrict it. In the process, he does not move toward anarchy, toward some sort of uncontrolled self-expressionism; he moves instead toward mastery of the full gamut of the techniques of traditional English prose. Nor does proficiency in the use of accepted techniques inhibit invention or inspiration; the way even to originality, perhaps particularly to originality, is through mastery of form.[1]

[1] Baxter Hathaway, *Writing Mature Prose—The Mastery of Sentence Structure* (New York: The Ronald Press Company, 1951), pp. iii–iv. Copyright 1951 The Ronald Press Company.

Professor Hathaway's straightforward approach to writing reminds one of Matthew Arnold's comment about style. When asked about the secret of style, Arnold replied, "Have something to say and say it as clearly as you can. That is the only secret of style."

With Matthew Arnold supplying the focus and Professor Hathaway the specific techniques, there is no reason why you cannot be a better writer as a sophomore than you were when a freshmen; and with continued desire, effort, and practice—to make good writing a habit— ". . . you should become a capable writer—not a brilliant one perhaps, since brilliance cannot easily be taught—but a writer capable of the competent kind of expression that is highly prized in the workaday world and never to be scorned even by the best literary craftsmen." [2]

[2] Baxter Hathaway, *Writing Mature Prose: The Mastery of Sentence Structure* (New York: The Ronald Press Company, 1951), p. 3. Copyright 1951 The Ronald Press Company.

Criteria for Good Writing

Baxter Hathaway

ONE "Correctness" can be taught by rules; "excellence" cannot be. To become an excellent writer, you must understand operating principles and guiding laws, but you must still use your own judgment, for no simple rules-of-thumb are sufficient. You must become a master of language and not a slave of it. Paradoxical as it may seem, the way to liberation is by submission to the forms and logic of language. Just as a plumber is free to be a good plumber only by mastering the tricks of his trade, so are you free to express yourself well only when you have learned enough of the specific techniques of expression to convey easily the full spread of the ideas in your mind. Set yourself the task . . . of mastering a limited number of techniques and of extending the repertoire of writing habits that you have at hand. In doing that, you need also to understand the logic behind the techniques so that you can judge for yourself when to employ them. . . .

TWO What then are the basic criteria for good writing? Here are a few. Come to understand them so that you can decide for yourself what effects you are particularly striving for in any writing that you do.

Unity

THREE Usually a writer has some one main idea that he is trying to communicate to his reader, and he arranges his materials to express and substantiate that idea. This principle can be put into forthright maxims:

1. Say one thing at a time.
2. Keep out of your writing anything that is irrelevant to the point you are making.
3. Point your evidence, examples, contributory ideas toward the main idea you are trying to express.
4. Do not put unlike ideas into the same sentence unless you can show clearly that in some broader way they belong together.
5. Do not put unlike ideas into the same paragraph unless you can show clearly that in some broader way they belong together.
6. Do not put unlike ideas into the same section of the whole unless you can show clearly that in some broader way they belong together.

FOUR Ideas belong together when some higher principle of organization that holds them together is evident to the reader. . . . Ideas that are placed together should, in other words, have tangible and evident relationship, and ordinarily nothing should be included within a piece of writing that does not support or lead toward the effect or idea that the writer would achieve. . . .

Continuity

FIVE Most writers try to achieve some kind of "flow" in their passages. One idea should run on into another idea. The reader should be able to sense a movement progressively in one direction. The idea should seem to walk, run, gallop.

SIX The enemies of continuity are short, choppy sentences, gaps in thought, excursions from the central lines of development, and absence of a sufficient number of the words that indicate transitions from one idea to the next—although, strictly speaking, the problems of transition belong to "coherence" and not to "continuity." Short sentences are not at fault in themselves for expert writers are often able to maintain a high degree of continuity with short sentences sustained over a long passage. If you as a writer can feel the continuity in what you have to say, you should be able without much trouble to cast your ideas into a form in which consecutive ideas naturally follow one another. Use common sense. . . .

SEVEN   To get continuity, you must consider the ideas that you are expressing, not as separate detached units, but as an organic whole moving in a certain direction. No sentence should be entirely in repose, entirely a balanced unit in itself, but should lean slightly toward the following sentence. Similarly each paragraph should lean toward, anticipate, reveal the force of attraction of the paragraph that follows it.

Coherence

EIGHT   Bind ideas together. Whenever there is a logical relationship between two or more ideas, you need some kind of "glue" or "chain" to attach them. Between some ideas the relationships are so close and firm that the writer needs to do nothing to make them stick together, as in the sentences: "You have harmed us. Now we distrust you." "The neighbor's cat just stole the hamburger from the back porch. Where is my shotgun?" But the ideas in most passages are not so clearly related, and you must furnish "glue" to attach them together. You may use words like "however," "therefore," "still," "yet," "even so," "furthermore" to show relationships. Or try repeating key words. Pronouns are useful as binding agents. Insert phrases that describe relationships. Most coherent writing contains a combination of all these. Any kind of subordinating or relating device is useful.

Clarity

NINE   Clarity in writing usually comes from clarity in thinking, from a recognition of the right relationships between the things to be said, and from an understanding of the common conventions as to what grammatical constructions accomplish and signify. A particularly important aid to clarity can be described figuratively as "keeping lines straight." Never make a casual shift in your approach to a subject. If you have laid claim to one peephole through which to look at your subject, do not shift to another without giving proper warning. Do not shift tenses without a reason for doing so. Do not shift from "you" to "one" or to "we," or vice versa, without reason. Never avoid a natural opportunity for parallel construction. . . .

Economy

TEN   . . . The principle of economy, stated briefly, is that no words should be used if the idea is just as clear and meaningful without them. Good writers do not waste words; they do not pad. You can test your writing for this quality most easily in individual sentences. Can you cut out any words and leave your meaning intact? Is every word worth the space it occupies? Flabbiness is the opposite of economy in writing. A good sentence is like a fighter in ring condition, with all excess fat worked off and every muscle and fiber an efficient engine to do the job that faces him. It is not simple necessarily; it is as complicated as the task to be done, but with no waste motion or parts. You should not bring into play an elaborate grammatical engine to move a small idea any more than you would use a steam shovel to move a pebble.

ELEVEN Cut out unnecessary little qualifying words that suck the vitality from your expressions. Let an experience be "good," not "quite good" or "rather good" or "more or less good." Do not build unnecessary scaffolds around your main ideas; what difference in meaning can you find between "*There are* some children *who* don't like ice cream" and "Some children don't like ice cream"? The "there are" construction here is an unnecessary scaffold added to the central idea. Do not duplicate expressions. Do not say, "Our annual visit once a year." Do you need both "crept" and "stealthily" in "He crept stealthily into the room"? These are all obvious matters of economy. . . .

Energy

TWELVE . . . Energy of writing supplies the momentum for the transmission of many difficult ideas across the barrier of a reader's in- attention. . . .

THIRTEEN Writers are something like pitchers in baseball. Some pitchers have control and no speed; others have plenty of speed but not enough control; the perfect pitcher has both. The quality in writing that corresponds to speed is energy. Control is expressed in writing principally in terms of unity, emphasis, and coherence.

FOURTEEN Above all, stay as close as you can to concrete language. Language is concrete when it refers to individual actions and individual persons and individual settings. One effective way of securing concrete- ness is to substitute the typical concrete object for an abstraction when it is possible to do so. Say "Judge Smith and Doctor Brown" instead of "professional men" if the more concrete phrase will communicate the full meaning of the reference. Keep your reader in touch with the world of the senses. At the same time keep your perceptions accurate and close to the frontier of thought, steel-bright. Good metaphors provide the life of much language.

FIFTEEN These qualities—unity, continuity, coherence, clarity, economy, and energy—are not the only qualities of good writing. The listing represents an artificial attempt to isolate some of the characteristics that may make one piece of writing better than another. It is false criticism to condemn a piece of writing for failure in one of these qualities when obvious effectiveness indicates that failure in one direction is more than compensated by excellence in another. Furthermore, virtues of any kind, as we know them, become vices in excess. But with these cautions it is safe to proceed to test the value of prose by these measuring sticks.

criteria for good writing

1. From the context, which of the following definitions is best for the word, *substantiate?* (Par. 3: ". . . he arranges his materials to express and *substantiate* that idea.")
   - a. liberate
   - b. verify
   - c. relate to
   - d. enlarge

2. Which of the following are among the enemies of continuity, according to Professor Hathaway?
   - a. long, complex sentences
   - b. long paragraphs
   - c. lack of transition words
   - d. incomplete thoughts

3. What purpose is served by the comparison of writers to pitchers in baseball?
   - a. to imply that writing is like a game
   - b. to emphasize the importance of practice
   - c. to indicate that good writing is important for everyone, even athletes
   - d. to clarify the qualities which a writer should possess

4. Which of the following phrases best describes the pattern of development?
   - a. an introduction followed by a series of unrelated topics on writing
   - b. an introduction followed by a series of related topics on writing
   - c. definition of subject, development by series of related topics, conclusion
   - d. definition of subject, development by series of unrelated topics, conclusion

5. Which of the following words is used by Professor Hathaway in an emotive sense?
   - a. excellent   (Par. 1: "To become an *excellent* writer, you must understand. . . .")
   - b. enemies   (Par. 6: "The *enemies* of continuity are short, choppy sentences. . . .")
   - c. logical   (Par. 8: "Whenever there is a *logical* relationship between two or more ideas. . . .")
   - d. criticism   (Par. 15: "It is false *criticism* to condemn a piece of writing. . . .")

6. Which of the following best describes the tone of this paper?
   - a. persuasive and serious

      b. impersonal and condescending

      c. didactic and condescending

      d. descriptive and humorous

7. Which of the following best describes the moral or philosophical attitude expressed in this paper?

      a. an excellent writer is a good individual

      b. a person who can't express his ideas lives a meaningless life

      c. clarity in writing implies an ordered life

      d. none of the above

8. Which of the following inferences seems most likely as a statement of the author's attitude toward the criteria for good writing?

      a. they are helpful but not necessary

      b. they are indispensable

      c. the lack of any or all of them usually lowers the paper's value

      d. he presents the generally accepted ideas about good writing but does not earnestly support them

9. What purpose is served by comparing a good sentence to a fighter in the ring?

      a. to simplify the concept of a good sentence

      b. to show the aggressiveness of a good sentence

      c. to further develop the preceding sentence

      d. to give an interesting example which the reader will remember

10. Which of the following best describes the author's intention in this paper?

      a. to scold poor writers

      b. to appear as an authority on writing

      c. to provide useful rules for writing

      d. to correct the ideas of other teachers of writing

11

comments

The Cliché Expert Takes the Stand

The purpose of this preface is to make all of us aware that some words have become so limp that they can no longer carry ideas which are forceful and insightful, no matter how loud we shout them, unless of course, we have the ingenuity of a Thurber; then, we can whisper them and they may be heard around the world.

Some argue that the cliché is an economical way, both in words and time, of getting an idea across. I agree that much meaning is compressed within the cliché, but the catch is that the meaning of such words does not carry a punch strong enough to burst through the barrier of the inattention and the mental preoccupation of the audience.

Now, I am not against economy in speech and writing; nor am I one who feels that what is "easy" is therefore bad. But, my point is that the easy cliché not only promotes passiveness in both speech and listening, but that it also numbs the thinking and listening processes. How terrible to contemplate that the mental processes, through inactivity, may lose resilience, and worse still, perhaps atrophy to some degree.

Let us counteract quickly this hardening process. The next time you are on the verge of uttering a cliché, suppress it and use other words. It may well be that the "other words" may not be so terse, but you'll find one big difference in making a *new* utterance. The difference is that you will *think*. To think, you must keep in mind the thought you wish to express, make choices among words to use, and best of all, you must process through the "brain cells" your speech, modes of speaking, and emphases.

Walter Pauk, "The Reading Expert Takes the Final Exam," *The Journal of the Reading Specialist*, 3, No. 3 (March 1964), pp. 40–41. Reprinted by permission of the publisher.

When you think as you speak (a fine habit to cultivate) you will experience a joy that you are now saying more nearly what you wanted to say. Actually, thinking-while-speaking is a creative process truly; whereas, there is little if any creative effort in the outpouring of clichés.

The clichés are, also, robbers of our thoughts and destroyers of our personalities because the words which flow glibly from our lips are not really ours—these counterfeit words seem to offer irresistible cues which make the next utterance follow the first, and the subsequent one the previous. It is somewhat like drifting unthinkingly into the wrong lane of traffic on a superhighway. Once you are in it, you are stuck. You have to stay there and keep moving. You end up where you did not want to go in the first place.

So with clichés, too, we find frequently that the outpouring words somehow gain control, leading to one cliché after another, one generality after another, each, so to speak, conjuring up the next. In the end, if one stopped to analyze such a conversation, the analysis would show: much verbiage, no direction. It is the *sine qua non* of communication that the thinking process—the thoughts—remain in control, and that the words express—make vital—our thoughts.

❀   ❀   ❀

AFTER-THOUGHT: Thinking while speaking is man at his best.

The Cliché Expert Takes the Stand

Frank Sullivan

Question. Mr. Arbuthnot, you are an expert in the use of the cliché, are you not?

Answer. Yes, sir, I am a certified public cliché expert.

Q. In that case would you be good enough to answer a few questions on the use and application of the cliché in ordinary speech and writing?

A. I should be only too glad to do so.

Q. Your occupation?

A. Well, after burning the midnight oil at an institution of higher

Frank Sullivan, "The Cliché Expert Takes the Stand, *The New Yorker*. Reprinted by permission; copyright © 1935, 1963 by The New Yorker Magazine, Inc.

learning, I was for a time a tiller of the soil. Then I went down to the sea in ships for a while, and later, at various times, I have been a guardian of the law, a gentleman of the Fourth Estate, a poet at heart, a bon vivant and raconteur, a prominent clubman and man about town, an eminent . . .

Q. Just what is your occupation at the moment, Mr. Arbuthnot?

A. At the moment I am an unidentified man of about forty, shabbily clad.

Q. How do you cliché experts reveal yourselves, Mr. Arbuthnot?

A. In our true colors, of course.

Q. And you expect to live to . . .

A. A ripe old age.

Q. What do you shuffle off?

A. This mortal coil.

Q. What do you thank?

A. My lucky stars.

Q. What kind of retreats do you like?

A. Hasty retreats.

Q. What do you do to hasty retreats?

A. I beat them.

Q. Regarding dogs, what kind of dog are you?

A. A gay dog.

Q. And how do you work?

A. Like a dog.

Q. And you lead?

A. A dog's life.

Q. So much for dogs. Now, Mr. Arbuthnot, when you are naked you are . . .

A. Stark naked.

Q. In what kind of daylight?

A. Broad daylight.

Q. What kind of outsider are you?

A. I'm a rank outsider.

Q. How right are you?

A. I am dead right.

Q. What kind of meals do you like?

A. Square meals.

Q. What do you do to them?

A. Ample justice.

Q. What is it you do to your way?

A. I wend my way.

Q. And your horizon?

A. I broaden my horizon.

Q. When you buy things, you buy them for . . .

A. A song.

Q. You are as sober as . . .

A. A judge.

Q. And when you are drunk?

A. I have lots of leeway there. I can be as drunk as a coot, or a lord, or an owl, or a fool . . .

Q. Very good, Mr. Arbuthnot. Now, how about the fate of Europe?

A. It is hanging in the balance, of course.

Q. What happens to landscapes?

A. Landscapes are dotted.

Q. What kind of precision are you cliché-users partial to?

A. Clocklike precision.

Q. And what kind of order?

A. Apple-pie order.

Q. When you watch a parade, you watch it from . . .

A. A point of vantage.

Q. And you shroud things . . .

A. In the mists of antiquity.

Q. What kind of threats do you make?

A. Veiled threats.

Q. And what kind of secrets do you betray?

A. Dark secrets.

Q. How about ignorance?

A. Ignorance is always abysmal.

Q. When you travel, what do you combine?

A. I combine business with pleasure.

Q. And you are destined . . .

A. To go far.

Q. Thank you, Mr. Arbuthnot. What time is it?

A. It is high time.

Q. How do you point?

A. I point with pride, I view with alarm, and I yield to no man.

Q. What do you pursue?

A. The even tenor of my way.

Q. Ever pursue the odd tenor of your way?

A. Oh, no. I would lose my standing as a cliché expert if I did that.

Q. As for information, you are . . .

A. A mine of information.

Q. What kind of mine?

A. A veritable mine.

Q. What do you throw?

A. I throw caution.

Q. Where?

A. To the winds.

the cliché expert takes the stand

1. From the context which of the following definitions is best for the word, "veritable"?
   a. real or truthful
   b. exact or precise
   c. ubiquitous or omnipotent
   d. essential or necessary

2. What attitude toward ignorance did Mr. Arbuthnot express?
   a. ignorance is greater than it should be
   b. ignorance is so great that it is immeasurable
   c. ignorance is foolishness
   d. ignorance is backwardness

3. What is the purpose of the figure of speech (simile) in which Arbuthnot calls his kind of order "apple pie order"?
   a. to explain that his order is as perfect and precise as an apple pie is perfectly delicious
   b. to explain that his order is as unorganized as the mixed-up and cooked together apples in a pie
   c. to explain that his order is of the "homemade" variety; in other words, a definite pattern of order exists, but it is his own "brand"
   d. to explain that he feels order is quite unnecessary, but desirable when possible; just as apple pie is an unnecessary but delicious desert

4. Which of the following phrases best describes the pattern of development of this passage?
   a. an interview with a cliché expert which reveals certain enumerated professional views about this peculiar profession
   b. a question and answer session with a cliché expert, with the answers presenting examples of the use and application of the cliché as answers to "set up" type questions
   c. a conversation between two cliché experts leading to conclusions about the use and application of clichés in conversation through the use of carefully worded questions which anticipate clichés for answers
   d. an interview in which the cliché expert discusses a series of diverse topics in detail without any overall direction to the interview

5. Which of the following words was used by Arbuthnot in an emotive sense?
   a. stark   ("*Stark* naked.")
   b. sober   ("You are as *sober* as . . .")
   c. rank   ("I'm a *rank* outsider.")
   d. alarm   ("I view with *alarm*.")

6. Which of the following best describes the tone of this interview?
   a. humorous for humor's sake

    b. humorous and cynical
    c. rhetorical with underlying irony
    d. figurative with a rhetorical purpose

7. Which of the following best describes the moral or philosophical attitude expressed in this interview?

    a. clichés serve as crutches for the unimaginative in conversations
    b. clichés, when carefully used, add spice to a conversation
    c. one has to be "set-up" with leading questions to be a successful cliché user
    d. the author did not reveal that any philosophical or moral attitude is most likely

8. Which inference is most likely from Arbuthnot's statement in which he claims to like "square meals"?

    a. he likes hearty meals
    b. he likes delicious meals
    c. he likes gourmet meals
    d. he likes balanced meals

9. What purpose is served by Arbuthnot's saying that he pursues the "even tenor" of his way?

    a. he holds to a continuous course whatever it may be
    b. he pursues the "low" road
    c. he pursues the "high" road
    d. he pursues a happy course

10. Which of the following best describes the author's intent in this interview?

    a. to show that most clichés are such widely known expressions that one can anticipate them in advance
    b. to summarize within one passage the current clichés of the day
    c. to satirize and poke fun at cliché users
    d. his intent was strictly to present slapstick humor for the benefit of the reader

part vi

On Writing the Research Paper

No matter how hard students try to write creative compositions of good quality, there will always be some who simply cannot manage to do so; but there should be no student who cannot write a research paper of good quality.

Research writing as contrasted to creative writing can be done, almost entirely, by following a system. In broad terms, here are the essential steps: (1) make sure that the topic you chose is one that you are deeply interested in; (2) check with your instructor to make certain that the topic is *narrow* enough to be handled in depth; (3) be sure that you find all of the pertinent references; (4) take clear, accurate, easily identifiable notes on every item which you believe will be useful; (5) use cards of uniform size, be certain to put only one item on each card, and use only one side of the card; (6) jot a topical heading for each item so that the cards can be easily categorized for the writing stage of the paper; (7) once categorized, shift the piles about to make up the best possible organization for the paper; (8) read over each pile of notes so thoroughly that when you begin writing, your thoughts, couched in your words will flow forth; and (9) revise the paper until you know it is the best you can do with the material at that time.

Brooks and Warren have much to offer in their paper. Read it carefully.

12

The Research Paper

Cleanth Brooks and Robert Warren

ONE   The research paper draws its material from many sources. Its aim is to assemble facts and ideas and by studying them to draw new conclusions as to fact or interpretation, or to present the material in the light of a new interest. For instance, a military historian who wanted to understand why General Lee lost the Battle of Gettysburg would study the written records of orders and events, the correspondence and memoirs of witnesses, the actual terrain, and the interpretations of other historians. In the light of that evidence, he would try to frame an explanation. Or a literary critic who wanted to understand why a certain novelist often used certain themes would study the facts of the novelist's life as found in whatever sources (letters, memoirs, public records, biographies), the kind of education he received, the kind of ideas current in his particular place and time, and so forth. Such material would be his evidence. The researcher might discover new facts, and new facts can easily upset old theories. But he might have to depend on facts which were already available but available in scattered sources. Then his task would be to collect those facts into a new pattern of interpretation.

TWO   The difference between the book written by the professional historian or literary critic and the term paper written by a student may appear so great that they seem to have no relation. But the basic method should be the same: to collect the facts and interpret them. The term paper can be intelligent, well informed, interesting, and original in its conclusions, and the student should try to make it so. But first of all he should try to make his work systematic. If it is not systematic it will probably not have the other qualities.

THREE The first step toward making his paper systematic is to learn how to investigate his subject. The historian going to the order book of a general, the documents of a politician, the terrain of a battle-field; the anthropologist observing the Indian tribe; or the literary scholar studying the manuscripts or letters of an author is using what are called primary sources. He goes to original sources of information for his facts. But the college student must usually use secondary sources. He reads the report of the anthropologist or he studies an edition of a poet prepared by a scholar. But even here there are degrees. He should try to use material which is as close as possible to the original source of information. He should not depend on digests or commentaries of the anthropologist's report, but should go to the report itself. He should not merely read what has been said about a novelist, but should read the novelist's actual work. He should not rely on interpretations of the Declaration of Inde-pendence, but should study the actual text. Get as close to the facts as possible. No matter how good your reasoning is, it is useless if the facts on which it works are not dependable.

FOUR The research paper, we have said, draws its material from many sources. It is not a digest of one book or article. But how do you get at the useful sources?

FIVE Special reference books give a good starting point, standard encyclopedias and dictionaries, and such compilations as the *American Yearbook,* the *Statesman's Yearbook,* and the *World Almanac.* In addi-tion to such general reference works, there are those devoted to special fields, for example, the *Dictionary of National Biography* (limited to the British), the *Dictionary of American Biography, Living Authors, Who's Who* (British), *Who's Who in America,* the *Encyclopedia of the Social Sciences,* the *Catholic Encyclopedia,* the *Cambridge History of English Literature,* the *Cambridge History of American Literature,* the *Oxford Companion to English Literature,* the *Oxford Companion to American Literature,* Bartlett's *Familiar Quotations,* and the *Reader's Guide to Periodical Literature.* Reference books are so numerous and sometimes so specialized that it is often helpful to consult the *Guide to Reference Books,* by I. G. Mudge, to know where to go in the first place.

SIX The reference book will give an introduction to a subject and certain basic facts. Best of all for the student, it will usually offer a list of other works, books or articles less limited in scope than the treatment in the reference book itself. With this as a starting point the student can make up his own *working bibliography* for his subject. As he reads into his subject he will encounter references to other works, and can gradually extend the range of his working bibliography. The subject catalogue of the library will also provide new items.

SEVEN The working bibliography should be kept on convenient cards of uniform size, with only one entry to a card. This allows the student to arrange them in alphabetical, or other order (by topics, for example), according to his need. The entry on the card should contain all the basic information about a book or article; the author's name with the last name first, the title of the work, the volume number if any, the place of publication, the publisher, the date of publication. If the work appears in a periodical or collection, that fact should be indicated with volume number, the date, and the pages occupied by the work.

EIGHT This form is to be retained in making up a final bibliography to be attached to your finished paper. There the order will be alphabetical by authors. Your final bibliography may be shorter than your working bibliography, for the final bibliography should contain no entry from which you have not taken material for the actual paper, whereas certain items in your working bibliography will be dropped as more valuable items come to light.

NINE The professional scholar may want to work through all the material on his subject, but the student preparing a term paper scarcely has the time for such a program. And many items in the bibliographies he encounters are antiquated or trivial. So to save his time and energy, he should try to select the items which will best repay his attention. There is no rule for this. Selected bibliographies sometimes appear in textbooks and other works. Sometimes an author will refer with special respect to another work on his subject. But the student can always take his working bibliography to an instructor and ask for comment.

TEN Unless you take notes on your reading you will probably not be able to remember much of the relevant material and will certainly not be able to organize it well when you come to write your paper. If you have taken your notes carefully, you will be able to lay out before you the whole subject and put it in order. The paper will almost write itself. But if the notes are to give you the most help, they must have a convenient mechanical form.

ELEVEN Notes can be put on note cards (usually 3" by 5"), on small or half sheets, or on full sheets. What you use does not much matter, so long as the size is manageable and uniform. As already mentioned, not more than one note, however brief, should be on a single card or sheet. This rule should be strictly adhered to, even when the notes are on the same topic; for when you take the notes, you cannot be sure in what order you will eventually use them. Only if each note is independent can you arrange them in the order desired when you come to write your paper. Each note should carry at the top, at left or toward the center, some indication of the precise content, not the general subject of your investigation, but some subtopic. And at the top right, or at the bottom, the note should carry an adequate reference to the source from which it is drawn. Presumably the full bibliographical information about that source is already in your working bibliography, and so some skeleton notation will be adequate here. . . .

TWELVE   So much for the mechanics of note taking. As for the process, you should make your notes relevant, accurate, and clear. To make them relevant you must keep constantly in mind the main purpose of your investigation. You are studying a particular subject with particular limits. You are not concerned with anything only casually associated with the subject. If, for instance, when your subject is the economic backgrounds of the American Revolution, you are reading a general history of the period, you should not be distracted by military strategy of the French and Indian Wars or an analysis of Puritan theology. Your job is to follow your main purpose through a body of various materials, and often what is major for you will be minor in the work you are investigating.

THIRTEEN   It is possible to take notes prematurely. Therefore, it is always best to become acquainted with a work before you take notes from it. In your first reading you may indicate material for possible notes, and pass on. When you have finished the work, or those parts relevant to your interest, you can then better assess the material for possible notes. In this way you will get from any particular work only the most pertinent notes, and you will avoid duplication.

FOURTEEN   The note itself may be direct quotation or summary. If direct quotation is used, it is sometimes valuable to record the context of the quotation. What leads the author to make his statement? What point does he try to establish by it? You do not want to misinterpret your author by implication. For instance, suppose a critic should write:

> Although Herman Melville has created in Captain Ahab of *Moby Dick* a character of intense interest and monumental proportions, he has in general little sense of the shadings of personality and motive. Most of his creations are schematic, mere outlines without flesh. He lacks that basic gift of the novelist, a sense of character.

If you, assembling material for a paper on Melville as a novelist, should merely quote, "Herman Melville has created in Captain Ahab of *Moby Dick* a character of intense interest and monumental proportions," you would have a misleading note. An accurate note would run something like this:

> Even though William — believes that Melville in general lacks a sense of character, he admits that Captain Ahab is a "character of intense interest and monumental proportions."

But this principle of context holds good for the note by summary as well as the note by quotation.

FIFTEEN When you are taking notes by summary, the kind of summary to be used depends on the special case. In one case, the author's method of reasoning may be very important, and then the summary should be of a form to indicate the logical structure of the original text. In another case, where mere facts or scattered opinions are involved, the summary need record merely these facts and opinions. As for the scale of the summary, there is no guiding principle except the note-taker's need. Try to forecast what you will need when you actually come to write your paper, not merely what you will want to incorporate in the paper but what you will need to understand your subject fully.

SIXTEEN Once your notes are taken, how do you use them? This again depends on the kind of subject you are dealing with. Some subjects suggest a chronological order, others a logical order. For instance, if you are doing a paper on Keats's development as a poet you might first arrange your notes chronologically—notes on early poems, notes on middle poems, notes on late poems. But if your subject is an analysis of the themes of Keats's poems, you might try to arrange your notes by themes, running various classifications until you had one that seemed to make sense. Or you might find, sometimes, that two levels of organization were necessary. For instance, certain themes of Keats's poems might be characteristic of certain periods. Then having established one type of classification (by theme) you might run another type (by chronology). Notes are flexible. You can use them as a device to help your thinking, or to help you organize your material.

SEVENTEEN Notes record questions and issues. The different authors you have consulted have had individual approaches to the general subject, different interests, different conclusions. As you work over your cards you can locate these differences and try to see what they mean to you in your special project. Ask yourself if there is any pattern of disagreement among the authors you have consulted. List the disagreements. Are they disagreements of fact or of interpretation? Compare the evidence and reasoning offered by the authors who are in disagreement. Can you think of any new evidence or new line of reasoning on disputed points? Can you think of any significant points not discussed by your authors? What bearing would such points have on their conclusions? Again, use your notes as a device to help your thinking.

EIGHTEEN By working over your notes and thinking about ideas suggested in them you will probably strike on some vague general plan for your paper. But do not commit yourself to the first plan that comes into your head. Consider various possibilities. Then when you have struck on the most promising, try to work up an outline on that basis.

You will undoubtedly start with a sort of rough suggestive outline, the barest shadow of the paper you want to write. By checking back on your material you can begin to fill in the outline and determine the relation among the facts and ideas you wish to present. So you will arrive at a more fully organized outline. Perhaps a topic outline will serve your purpose, but at some stage a sentence outline will probably be helpful, for to make it you will have to state clearly exactly what you mean.

NINETEEN   Once you have an outline prepared you can begin the actual composition. Use your outline as a guide, but do not consider yourself bound by it. As you write, new ideas will probably come to you, and if they are good ideas you should revise your outline to accommodate them. The outline is not sacred. Like your notes, it is simply a device to help you think. And remember that your paper should be a fully rounded composition, unified and coherent, emphasizing matters according to the scale of their importance. The outline is only a start toward creating a balanced, fluent, well-proportioned discussion.

TWENTY   Your paper should be more than a tissue of facts and quotations from your notes. It should represent your handling of a subject and not a mere report on what other writers have said. Naturally, a large part of your material will be derived from other writers, but you should always ask yourself just what a fact or idea means in terms of your own purpose. It should find a place in your pattern, and if there is no proper place for it, it should be excluded. In the end, you will always find that some of your notes are not usable. A writer who has studied his subject always has more material than he can well use.

TWENTY-ONE   Full credit should be given for the source of every fact or idea derived from another writer. In your own text you will want to acknowledge any important item as a matter of help to your reader. It is easy to introduce a statement or a quotation by a clear explanatory phrase or sentence. We are all accustomed to such introductory remarks as these:

Charles A. Beard has proved that . . .

James Truslow Adams maintains that . . .

An excellent statement of this view is given by James Truslow Adams in his *Epic of America:* . . .

As Sinclair Lewis shows in *Main Street,* the culture of the American town is . . .

On the other hand, such a liberal as Henry A. Wallace holds that . . .

As Thomas Wolfe observed . . .

Some facts or ideas can simply be stated in your text if the fact or idea is not specially to be associated with the particular writer from whom you derived it. But in all cases, authority should be given in a footnote.

the research paper

1. From the context of the article you have just read, which of the following best describes a research paper?

     a. a representative compilation and reorganization of facts and quotations on note cards

     b. a paper which presents all aspects of the subject and neither explicitly nor implicitly endorses any one

     c. a creative fling at a subject which, though based on conjecture and chance, often unearths many important ideas

     d. the original interpretation of a subject based on a knowledge of the factual material associated with it

2. Which of the following would not be a useful aid in finding reference materials?

     a. *Familiar Quotations*

     b. *Dictionary of American Biography*

     c. *Readers' Digest*

     d. *Readers' Guide to Periodical Literature*

3. What is meant by the statement, "Your paper should be more than a *tissue* of facts"? (Paragraph 20).

     a. your paper should not be written on tissue paper; it wrinkles too easily

     b. your paper should not merely contain tissue facts, that is, facts that should be discarded once they have been read

     c. your paper should not be a mere copy of the original thinker's ideas

     d. the paper you finally hand in should not be the carbon copy, but the original

4. Which of the following phrases best describes the pattern of development of this passage?

     a. description of how to write a research paper by the example of one on Melville

     b. a roundabout refutation and reorganization of the traditional method of writing a research paper

     c. an organized list of helpful sources for research

     d. prescription of chronological steps for writing a research paper

5. Which of the underlined words is used by the author in an emotive sense?

     a. (Par. 1: "But he might have to depend on facts which were already available but available in scattered sources.")

     b. (Par. 3: "The historian going to the order book of a general, the documents of a politician, the terrain. . . .")

     c. (Par. 9: "And many items in the bibliographies he encounters are antiquated or trivial.")

     d. (Par. 20: "Your paper should be more than a tissue of facts and quotations from your notes.")

6. Which of the following best describes the tone of this passage?
    a. impersonal and argumentative
    b. satirical and impersonal
    c. logical and moral
    d. impersonal and descriptive

7. Which of the following best describes the author's attitude regarding students' term papers?
    a. students should be given a course on writing term papers before they are asked to write one
    b. term papers are best written with little or no research but with a great deal of thought
    c. students do not have enough time to learn everything about a topic before writing on it
    d. students write poor papers because they lack initiative to do extensive research

8. Which of the following inferences can most logically be drawn from this essay?
    a. the writers thought Melville was a great writer and unjustly torn down by critics
    b. the best term papers are always typed with a carbon copy
    c. the student need not always footnote ideas that are not originally his own
    d. a term paper involves much more than merely reading one book about a subject and then immediately writing a final draft by restating the residue of facts from the reading

9. What purpose is served by the long list of reference sources?
    a. the writers want to show familiarity with the books in order to give the reader the impression that they are experts on research papers
    b. to plead for Melville on the grounds that all these writers agree that Melville is great
    c. to be specific and helpful rather than general and vague
    d. to make students aware of the many reference books available and the great variety of areas they cover

10. Which of the following best describes the author's intention in this passage?
    a. to provide a method or technique for students writing term papers
    b. to argue that notetaking is an important phase of writing a paper
    c. to give students a ready list of reference sources
    d. to imply that students should not take courses that require research papers

part vii

On Taking Notes

There are many opinions on how to take notes on a classroom lecture. Some say, "Put down your pencils and just listen." Others say, "Take only what seems important." My advice to students is: "Take copious notes—write as much as you have time for."

Before evaluating any of the above statements, a cogent reason for taking notes should be postulated. To preclude a long discussion, it seems to me that we take notes to record the lecturer's ideas in the sequence in which he presents them both for immediate and future reference.

In addition, the following well-known fact about memory should clinch the argument for taking copious notes: After a passage of two weeks' time, we forget about 90 per cent of the ideas that we have heard.

Think how important are copious notes for the college student who listens to three or four lectures a day, and who is quizzed every two weeks, then examined intensely at mid-semester, and examined again at the end of the semester, but this time for about three hours on each subject.

At the rate of 15 lectures a week, during a 15 week

semester, most students listen to well over 200 lectures during a
semester. Woe to the one who does not have full and accurate notes!

Then, too, there is the job of taking good notes on textbooks as
well as on reference books located in the libraries.

In taking notes on textbooks and other readings, one must be
wary about falling into these two traps:

First, don't take so many notes that you will be, in fact, rewriting the textbook. Such a mechanical procedure will rob you of
valuable time. Furthermore, note-taking does not necessarily result
in learning. The especially negative aspect of recording too many
notes is the almost impossible task of memorizing or learning them so
that the information can be used in class and for examinations.

Second, don't make the opposite mistake by making the notes
too short; you will find them difficult to decipher after a few weeks
go by. The notes should be in such a form that you can understand
them directly and immediately.

The best system for taking notes on textbooks is provided by
Professor Fox in the second selection in this part.

13

comments

Michael Faraday
On the Art of Taking Notes

Michael Faraday followed a procedure for taking notes that was bound to lead to success. Whether or not he was aware of it, he was, nevertheless, following certain principles of learning that are effective; for example, (a) taking full notes on every idea in the order of presentation; (b) making a second set of notes from the original notes immediately or shortly after the lecture while the lecturer's ideas are still relatively fresh in mind; (c) writing a lecture out in prose form to perceive it as a complete unit; and (d) rewriting a lecture in final form, to provide a prime opportunity for review.

Another technique for "capturing" the lecturer's ideas is contained in these words: ". . . in the composing of it I was aided by the ideas raised in my mind at the lecture . . ." (Par. 7). This comment, alluding to the prose draft, shows that Michael Faraday must have reflected on the ideas presented by the lecturer in the days which followed. There is, perhaps, no technique more valuable to scholarship than *reflection*— going over in one's mind the ideas expressed in a previous lecture. It is during the process of reflection that you really make the ideas, lately heard, your own.

Faraday's system for taking notes shows the great amount of time, effort and practice that must go into the process of truly *mastering* a lecture—mastering it so well that the knowledge becomes a springboard for creative thinking.

Though Faraday's system is sound, no student, carrying a full academic load, has time enough to rewrite lectures three times as did Faraday.

My suggestion is this: extract the benefit from the mental processes that Faraday went through, but do not do the rewriting of lectures. How can you do that, you probably are asking? Well, here is a time-proven, field-tested system.

To prepare for the taking of notes in a lecture, I suggest that you draw a line down the left side of your paper so that your paper will have a two-inch margin. If you use the standard size sheets (8½ x 11 inches), you will have a full 6 inches for recording the lecture notes.

STEP 1:   Take notes continually. Try to capture as much of the lecture as possible. Make an effort to write or print legibly.

Faraday's system: Faraday's method was, also, to record all the ideas presented by the lecturer.

STEP 2:   Directly after the lecture, especially if you have a free hour; or, that same evening at the latest, look over your notes while the lecturer's words are still ringing in your mind to fill in any gaps left in your notes.

Faraday's system: On the same evening of the lecture, or the next day at the latest, Faraday would re-copy his lecture notes, filling in gaps, but keeping the same format and contents of what transpired in the lecture. Essentially, he made a "clean" copy of his lecture notes. Again, the systems are very similar.

STEP 3:   After filling in any existing gaps, your next move is to use the two-inch column for making ever-so-brief jottings of the main ideas captured in your notes.

Faraday's system: Nothing comparable in Faraday's system.

STEP 4:   Now, take a blank sheet of paper and cover the notes—the notes on the 6-inch portion of the paper—leaving exposed the jottings in the 2-inch column. Then, using the jotting as clues or "flags," begin reciting aloud the main ideas of the lecture. Don't recite rotely, rather, use your own words, speaking in good grammatical sentences. Act as if you are reciting to the class.

Faraday's system: Faraday rewrote the lecture in as good grammatical form as he could, using his "raw" notes as the basis. You are doing a similar act, except that you are reciting rather than writing. Actually, you are getting more out of the lecture, at this stage, than Faraday probably did. You see, you are *recalling* the contents of the lecture without looking at your full notes. *Recalling*, as you probably know, is one of the most powerful steps in memorizing.

STEP 5:   Whenever you wish to review the lecture, either for an exam, or for the mastery of the subject, your notes are ready. Using the jottings in the 2-inch margin, you will be benefitting from the process of *recall* again and again.

Faraday's system: This step is comparable to Faraday's writing out the lecture in its final form. Actually, Faraday was using the lecture notes as a basis for writing his own personal textbook.

By following these five steps [1] for taking and studying lecture notes, you will be getting as much, if not more, than Faraday did, and in only a fraction of the time.

[1] Walter Pauk, *How to Study in College* (Boston: Houghton Mifflin Company, 1962), pp. 20–30.

On the Art of Taking Notes

Michael Faraday

ONE   Michael Faraday was born in September, 1791, in Newington Butts, Surrey, the second son of a journeyman blacksmith. At the age of 14 he was apprenticed to a bookbinder in London and during the term of his apprenticeship learned his trade, and the art of manipulation, well. Faraday was consumed by a passion for knowledge and in 1810 joined a group of other young men similarly inclined. This group, called the City Philosophical Society, met every Wednesday evening to listen to lectures given by the members. The senior member, a Mr. John Tatum, had a small collection of scientific apparatus, had published a few minor papers on electricity, and gave a whole series of lectures on the various sciences. It was at the City Philosophical Society that Faraday received his primary education in science. The passage that follows was written in the bound volume of his notes to a lecture on geology delivered by Tatum on February 17, 1811. It is to be found in the Faraday Manuscript Collection of the Royal Institution, London.

L. Pearce Williams, *Michael Faraday* (London: Chapman and Hall, Ltd., 1965; New York: Basic Books, Inc., Publishers, 1965). Reprinted by permission of the author. The remainder of this article is reproduced with the permission of the Royal Institution from Faraday's manuscript notes on a lecture on geology delivered by Mr. Tatum February 17, 1811.

TWO I have thought proper for several reasons to annex to this lecture the notes that I took at the delivery of it and also the second set of notes which I usually transcribed from the first at my return from the lecture room and had the idea entered my mind sooner, I should have done so to all the former lectures.

THREE My reasons are first that I may at any future period refer to them and notice in what manner I had taken the lecture off and what was the plan that I had pursued and secondly that I might either through inclination, for pleasure or any other cause compare the notes with the lecture and observe in what they correspond and in what they are faulty. But as my intention is to call to mind and memory at a future date what has now lately passed, that intention would not be answered completely by the notes alone, for to make it perfect it must be accompanied by a description of the manner in which these notes were taken and the method I pursued to draw up the lecture from them.

FOUR My method was to take with me a sheet or two of paper stitched or pinned up the middle so as to form something like a book. I usually got a front seat and there placing my hat on my knees and my paper on the hat I, as Mr. Tatum proceeded on in his lecture, set down the most prominent words, short but important sentences, titles of the experiments, names of what substances came under consideration, and many other hints that would tend to bring what had passed to my mind. Of this kind are the first set of notes belonging to this lecture and commencing a few pages further on. They are an exact copy of those that I took at the lecture except in being much more legible (I wrote with a pencil at the lecture) and better written and also certain long words that were only half wrote in the original notes are here given at full length.

FIVE On leaving the lecture room I proceeded immediately homewards and in that and the next night had generally drawn up a second set of notes from the first. These second notes were more copious, more connected and more legible than the first. The second set of notes belonging to this lecture is subjoined and by comparing them with the first, the improved state of them will be evident.

SIX These second set of notes were my guide whilst writing out the lecture in a rough manner. They gave me the order in which the different parts came under consideration and in which the experiments were performed and they called to mind the most important subjects that were discussed. I then referred to memory for the matter belonging to each subject and I believe I have not let much of the meaning and sense of Mr. Tatum's lectures slip. (I allude to the latter ones.)

SEVEN As I ultimately referred to memory for the whole of the lecture, it is not to be supposed that I could write it out in Mr. Tatum's own words. I was obliged to compose it myself but in the composing of it I was aided by the ideas raised in my mind at the lecture and I believe I have (from following my pattern as closely as I could) adopted Mr. Tatum's style of delivery to a considerable degree (perhaps no great acquisition).

EIGHT But tho' I have not wrote the lecture in Mr. Tatum's own words, the principles that were delivered in it are unalterable, and as I have been extremely careful in adhering to and giving those principles that Mr. Tatum laid down, the lectures are not materially different from those that were delivered by him. My meaning and sense is the same as his but we have expressed ourselves in different words.

NINE In addition to the lecture, when I had wrote one out, I always added at the end descriptions of the various experiments belonging to it. These opinions are pretty correct, for as I adopted every experiment as it was made and fixed it firmly in my mind, I found no difficulty in writing an account of them.

TEN But the case was different with respect to the outlined sketches that accompany some of the experiments. It would have occupied too much time to have made them a first and then a second time (as I have done with the lectures) and therefore I did not introduce them until I wrote the lecture out a second and last time in as perfect a state as I could. This second copy of the lecture is the present—taken from the first copy and the asperities and roughing rubbed off as well as I was able.

ELEVEN Let it here be observed that I know nothing of drawing, that is to say, I never learned it in a regular and proper manner. I have at times applyed a chance hour to the copying of prints, but that is very different from the delineating at some future time things that have been seen for perhaps half an hour. Yet this was my case, for some of the sketches have been made above nine weeks after the lecture was delivered and therefore my only method was to put together a few lines and those such as I thought would represent something like what I had seen.

TWELVE Under all these disadvantages, added to one of much greater consequence—namely the want of time (for I could seldom appropriate more than an hour or an hour and a half of each day to their purpose)—was this and all the former lectures composed, and therefore should any other person except myself read them, they will upon due consideration find, I hope, ample excuse for the numerous faults with which they abound.

on the art of taking notes

1. From the content which of the following definitions is the best for the word, *asperities?* (Par. 10: "This second copy of the lecture is the present —taken from the first copy and the *asperities* and roughing rubbed off as well as I was able.")

> a. roughness
> b. discordance
> c. sharpness
> d. crudeness

2. When did Faraday add the sketches of experiments to his copy?

> a. when he wrote the lecture out the last time
> b. as they were presented with the experiment
> c. as he took his first set of notes
> d. as he first wrote out the lecture

3. How did Faraday call to mind the most important subjects that had been discussed?

> a. from memory
> b. from his original notes
> c. from his second set of notes
> d. by going over his final copy of the lecture

4. Which of the following phrases best describes the pattern of development of the passage?

> a. several examples with comments
> b. statement followed by illustrative example
> c. several examples followed by a conclusion
> d. description to point out a moral

5. Which of the following words is used in an emotive sense?

> a. chance hour   (Par. 11: "I have at times applyed a *chance hour* to the copying of prints . . .")
> b. full length   (Par. 4: ". . . also certain long words that were only half wrote in the original notes are here given at *full length*.")
> c. for pleasure   (Par. 3: ". . . that I might either through inclination, *for pleasure* or any other cause compare the notes with the lecture . . .")
> d. rough manner   (Par. 6: "These second set of notes were my guide whilst writing out the lecture in a *rough manner*.")

6. Which of the following best describes the tone of the passage?

> a. moralistic and descriptive
> b. descriptive and argumentative
> c. logical and descriptive
> d. logical and rhetorical

7. Which of the following best describes the moral and philosophical attitude expressed in this passage?

> a. a man's personality is reflected in his behavior
> b. a man's personality affects his approach to problems
> c. being systematic is a virtue
> d. understanding his approach to learning is necessary for understanding a true scholar

8. Which of the following inferences seems most likely as an explanation of the phrase, "perhaps no great acquisition"?

> a. to understand Mr. Tatum's lecture was not of much importance

  b. Mr. Tatum's greatest skill was not his style of delivery
  c. to have his own copy of Mr. Tatum's lecture was not of much importance
  d. the experiments were not of much signficance to the lecture

9. What purpose is served by the description of Faraday's method of taking notes?

  a. it provides a good model to follow
  b. it shows how to put a logical plan into action
  c. it shows how a complete picture can be rebuilt by working from key ideas
  d. none of the above

10. Which of the following best describes the author's intention in this passage?

  a. to present students with a good method for taking notes
  b. to explain the operation of the City Philosophical Society
  c. to describe the kind of man Faraday was
  d. to explain how true mastery takes place

14

comments

On Taking Reading Notes

May I call your attention especially to the heart of the system for taking notes on textbooks: each paragraph bearing a main idea should be condensed to a sentence. Making a single sentence summary of each paragraph is more than a record of the author's main ideas: these notes will be a record of your interpretation of his main ideas.

Be aware too, that if such note-taking is done with great thought, you will be mastering the subject as well as preparing yourself for future quizzes and examinations.

How good it is, also, to push aside the heavy textbooks, bearing thousands of finely printed pages, and concentrate only on the several sheaves of notes to recapture the subject as you study for the final examination. Good notes provide a valuable reference which may be used as a basis for other courses taken in subsequent semesters. In later years, too, you may want to continue your education by reviewing these notes; or you may review to enjoy again the course as it unfolds in your well-kept notes.

You may retort to the final suggestion, "If I pass the course, I don't want to see those notes again." There are, however, many students who value their courses—who value learning. These students are those who really become *involved* in their studies and grow fond of learning and do not want forgetfulness to erode beyond recognition that which they spent so many hours in studying and learning in the first place. Such students, of course, strive for more than a diploma.

On Taking Reading Notes

Edward W. Fox

Historical Methods

ONE History, whether it is being studied by mature scholars or by beginning college students, involves the reading of a basic record (be it an assigned text or painstakingly assembled bits of source material), the ordering of the information it contains first into logical categories and eventually into meaningful propositions, and, if it is to be more than an antiquarian form of escape, the application of such propositions to current questions of political, moral, or intellectual significance. This means that the student must read the assigned text carefully and critically, and that, in addition to understanding what he has read, he must retain in his mind both the general propositions offered and the major facts upon which they are based.

TWO Important as this is, it is only the first part of his obligation as a student of history. He should then be prepared to test the general propositions he has encountered by applying them to new materials and also attempt to order new data to the development of new propositions. Translated into specific terms, this means that the student must take careful notes both of the required reading and of the lectures. The basic technique involved is that of summarization or the systematic condensation of each paragraph of the text to a sentence in his notes. It means further that he must be prepared to reverse the initial procedure and develop, or criticize, a proposition (offered in an examination) in a coherent and well-documented essay. *That is to say that the writing of an essay is a reversal of the process of taking notes, and that both are closely related to the basic process of historical thinking.*

Reading Notes

THREE In its simplest terms, taking notes on printed material involves the extraction from the text of a summary which corresponds to the outline or structure on which the author wrote the book. A practical approach to this end is to summarize in single concise sentences the major paragraphs in the assigned passage. The development of this technique

Edward W. Fox, *Syllabus for History* (Ithaca, New York: Cornell University, 1959), pp. 11–19. Reprinted by permission of the author.

demands concentrated application and steady practice, but, once mastered, it amply repays the student for his effort, not only by the efficient production of useful notes but also by increasing his critical powers of evaluation and judgment. He will find, for example, that this exercise will, more than anything else, improve his sense of the relative importance of the various facts and details presented in the reading.

FOUR Notes taken in paragraph form on a page with a wide left-hand margin are the most generally useful. *Elaborate arrangements tend to confuse, and the traditional topical form, the use of Roman numerals, capital letters, Arabic numerals, and small letters, etc., with much indentation, has a fatal tendency to imply a logical analysis rather than elicit one.* The most useful aspect of the topical outline can be added by annotation in the process of review. Topical headings, brief lists of points, and critical comments may be penciled in the margin of the notes during review in preparation for an examination. Most students find this an effective device. It forces them to select and extract the most important points, to keep their attention closely focused on the material, and to fix material in their minds through the mechanical process of writing it in summary form.

FIVE EXAMPLE: (The following, the work of a student in the course, will serve to illustrate the method suggested above. Note that he began by copying the author's name, title of the book, and the chapter number.)

Harry M. Orlinsky, *Ancient Israel*, Chap. I: "Fertile Crescent: Hebrew Origins"

6000–4500
People changed
from cave dwellers
to farmers in
F.C. & established
1st empires and
cities

The Fertile Crescent, a fertile area surrounded by the Tigris & Euphrates and extending from Syria to the Nile delta, was the site of man's first attempts at civilization. During the late Stone Age (6000–4500 B.C.) people changed from cave dwellers to farmers and herdsmen living in villages. Various metallurgical discoveries accelerated this process of social organization, and the many developments of this period include bronze, silver, lead, tin bronze (after 3000 B.C.), the wheel, & the plough. During the early bronze age (3000–2000 B.C.) people shifted about, as population increased (Sumer, Akkad & Egypt emerged). Cities developed, irrigation came into use, monumental structures, & writing (pictographic & cuneiform) began.

Societies with
political units

"City-States" developed from cities, and government in the form of assemblies of adult

& govt's	freemen (no women, children or slaves) came
developed	with them; also slavery as an economic in-
Slavery came	stitution (earlier slaves—captives of war). In
into being	due course kings (and then dynasties or kingly
	lines) & law codes (2 dating from 1950 B.C.,
	before Hammurabi, now found) came into
	being.

SIX   This being the first assignment of the year, the student took more complete and more formal notes than would be necessary later on. After a few weeks the beginner will find that he can select with more accuracy, make his style more telegraphic and abbreviate more frequently, as can be seen in the following examples taken from the work of the same student on the assignment of the third week:

SEVEN   Chester G. Starr, Jr., *The Emergence of Rome,* Chap. I: "Geography and Peoples of Ancient Italy"

Italy occupies central position in Med. & only purely Med. state to claim title of "great power." Geographically It. divided into peninsular It. & N. It. It is all hills with Apennines the main mts. It. has Med. climate modified in her favor.

EIGHT   *The Renaissance of Agriculture:* It.'s terrain & climate favors agriculture. Deposits enough to serve ancient world but that's all. Main riches of It. are forests, which were already shrunk by Christ's time, & fields & pasture. Sheep and goats are mainly raised and moved in a normal cycle for grazing. Ag. is chief pursuit, but most done from Sept. to May except grapes & olives. Ancient ag. required tremendous work & manpower. It. is a power well fit to rule the Med. world, but hard to unify within.

NINE   *Early Peoples:* It.'s "dawn of hist." is 700 B.C. In an iron age & population is from 4 main stocks & result of invasion. 1st came from N. Africa in 5000 B.C. & were shepherds & physical type of Its. today. In 2000 B.C. 2nd came across Alps & was part of movement of Indo-European speaking base for It. culture. By 700 these had merged in agricultural, animistically religious society of villages grouped into cantons who felt common bonds but also fought. By 700 Greek Etruscans arrived from E. Med. with far more advanced culture.

TEN   Because of the necessarily personal nature of note taking, no samples can be considered perfect models; ultimately they must be judged by their results. The merits of those given above are that they obviously result from a process of summarization and that, in spite of telegraphic style, they preserve the basic elements of sentence structure.

on taking reading notes

1. From the context, which of the following words do you think is best for
the word *animistically?* (Par. 9: "By 700 these had merged in agricultural,
animistically religious society of villages grouped into cantons who felt
common bonds but also fought.")
   - a. these people hated religion
   - b. these ancient people worshipped animals
   - c. the society was energetic and lively
   - d. these people believed the rocks and trees had souls

2. The author says that a summary should be extracted from the text and
detailed in the left margin using:
   - a. key words
   - b. concise sentences
   - c. main ideas
   - d. headings of topical outline

3. A rhetorical figure of speech called *periphrasis* is the term we use to
describe what an author does when he uses a roundabout way of writing
or a lengthy way of expressing something which could be said more
simply. Which of the following phrases could you condense into one word?
   - a. studied by mature scholars
   - b. the initial procedure
   - c. summarize in single concise sentences
   - d. retain in his mind

4. Which of the following phrases best describes the author's pattern of
development of this selection?
   - a. examples and comments on them
   - b. an introduction, list of rules, and a conclusion
   - c. description of a method followed by sample applications of
this method
   - d. a rambling description interspersed with personal ancedotes

5. The following phrases are listed in the order in which they appear in
Pars. 1 & 2. Look them up in their contexts and select the letter of the
one which seems most clearly designed to arouse your emotion.
   - a. (Par. 1, sentence 1)—mature scholars or beginning college
students
   - b. (Par. 1, sentence 1)—logical categories and meaningful
propositions
   - c. (Par. 1, sentence 2)—the student must read and must retain
   - d. (Par. 2, sentence 3)—the required reading and the lectures

6. Which of the following seems to be the best phrase to describe the tone
of Professor Fox's statement?
   - a. impersonal and rhetorical
   - b. logical and didactic
   - c. serious and descriptive
   - d. argumentative and didactic

7. Which of the following best describes the theme expressed in this selection?
    a. critical thinking is an important aspect of studying history
    b. the student should summarize and analyze
    c. to summarize is to learn
    d. notes must be taken to complete sentences

8. What does the author imply that the student will learn if he studies in the suggested manner?
    a. how the ancient Israelites lived
    b. how to take notes
    c. how to apply something he learns to something new he encounters
    d. how to develop his own abbreviations for taking notes

9. What is the author's purpose in including the notes taken on Orlinsky's book?
    a. it helps us learn about the beginning of community life
    b. it shows how long our notes should be
    c. it shows that notes can be shortened
    d. it shows what one student found to be important and how he cued himself

10. The author's intent in this selection is to:
    a. get students to take complete notes
    b. show the student how to take notes and how to use them in order to learn and to evaluate
    c. have students learn about historical methods
    d. emphasize that the student must do three things: read, listen in lecture, and take notes

part viii

On Laboratory Sciences

"Science is a romantic and wonderful game," said Kenneth Greisen, Professor of Physics (Nuclear Studies) at Cornell. He believes that if the excitement of the game could fire the imagination of the student, then the student would not need to read a book on how to study, for his enthusiasm would provide the momentum to carry him through at a high pitch. But Professor Greisen knows that such enthusiasm does not usually come about automatically. From years of experience, he concludes, "All too often, however, the beginning of study of an unfamiliar subject is difficult and painful, and students turn away from a potentially pleasurable subject in discouragement."

Professor Greisen's remark leads into the idea expressed in the selection about Professor Agassiz as a teacher. The selection develops the idea that the initial stages of any new subject or field are difficult to comprehend and master. What appears, at first, to be ordinary and, perhaps, without depth, frequently merits continued study when the perceiver knows what to look for and how to look.

How much easier, and how much more enjoyable

and profitable college work would be if every course were looked upon as an opportunity to explore, to understand, to learn. Though such a statement may seem idealistic, it may be viewed also as crassly pragmatic; that is, if you want good grades with the least amount of emotional turmoil, simply "love" every course you take. (This is not meant to be a facetious remark.)

15

In the Laboratory with Agassiz

Samuel H. Scudder

ONE   It was more than fifteen years ago that I entered the laboratory of Professor Agassiz, and told him I had enrolled my name in the scientific school as a student of natural history. He asked me a few questions about my object in coming, my antecedents generally, the mode in which I afterwards proposed to use the knowledge I might acquire, and, finally, whether I wished to study any special branch. To the latter I replied that while I wished to be well grounded in all departments of zoology, I purposed to devote myself specially to insects.

TWO   "When do you wish to begin?" he asked. "Now," I replied.

THREE   This seemed to please him, and with an energetic "Very well," he reached from a shelf a huge jar of specimens in yellow alcohol.

FOUR   "Take this fish," said he, "and look at it: we call it a Haemulon; by and by I will ask you what you have seen."

FIVE   With that he left me, but in a moment returned with explicit instructions as to the care of the object entrusted to me.

SIX   "No man is fit to be a naturalist," said he, "who does not know how to take care of specimens."

SEVEN   I was to keep the fish before me in a tin tray, and occasionally moisten the surface with alcohol from the jar, always taking care to replace the stopper tightly. Those were not the days of ground glass stoppers, and elegantly shaped exhibition jars; all the old students will recall the huge, neckless glass bottles with their leaky, wax-besmeared corks, half eaten by insects and begrimed with cellar dust. Entomology was a cleaner science than ichthyology, but the example of the professor who had unhesitatingly plunged to the bottom of the jar to produce the

Samuel H. Scudder, *Every Saturday* (April 4, 1874).

fish was infectious; and though this alcohol had "a very ancient and fishlike smell," I really dared not show any aversion within these sacred precincts, and treated the alcohol as though it were pure water. Still I was conscious of a passing feeling of disappointment, for gazing at a fish did not commend itself to an ardent entomologist. My friends at home, too, were annoyed, when they discovered that no amount of eau de cologne would drown the perfume which haunted me like a shadow.

EIGHT　In ten minutes I had seen all that could be seen in that fish, and started in search of the professor, who had, however, left the museum; and when I returned, after lingering over some of the odd animals stored in the upper apartment, my specimen was dry all over. I dashed the fluid over the fish as if to resuscitate it from a fainting fit, and looked with anxiety for a return of a normal, sloppy appearance. This little excitement over, nothing was to be done but return to a steadfast gaze at my mute companion. Half and hour passed, an hour, another hour; the fish began to look loathsome. I turned it over and around; looked it in the face—ghastly; from behind, beneath, above, sideways at a three-quarter view—just as ghastly. I was in despair; at an early hour I concluded that lunch was necessary; so with infinite relief, the fish was carefully replaced in the jar, and for an hour I was free.

NINE　On my return, I learned that Professor Agassiz had been at the museum, but had gone and would not return for several hours. My fellow students were too busy to be disturbed by continued conversations. Slowly I drew forth that hideous fish, and with a feeling of desperation again looked at it. I might not use a magnifying glass; instruments of all kinds were interdicted. My two hands, my two eyes, and the fish; it seemed a most limited field. I pushed my fingers down its throat to see how sharp its teeth were. I begin to count the scales in the different rows until I was convinced that that was nonsense. At last a happy thought struck me—I would draw the fish; and now with surprise I began to discover new features in the creature. Just then the professor returned.

TEN　"That is right," said he; "a pencil is one of the best eyes. I am glad to notice, too, that you keep your specimen wet and your bottle corked."

ELEVEN　With these encouraging words he added, "Well, what is it like?"

TWELVE　He listened attentively to my brief rehearsal of the structure of parts whose names were still unknown to me: the fringed gill-arches and movable operculum; the pores of the head, fleshy lips, and lidless eyes; the lateral line, the spinous fins, and forked tail; the compressed and arched body. When I had finished, he waited as if expecting more, and then with an air of disappointment,—

THIRTEEN　"You have not looked very carefully; why," he continued, more earnestly, "you haven't even seen one of the most conspicuous features of the animal, which is as plainly before your eyes as the fish itself; look again, look again!" And he left me to my misery.

FOURTEEN   I was piqued; I was mortified. Still more of that wretched fish! But now I set myself to my task with a will, and discovered one new thing after another, until I saw how just the professor's criticism had been. The afternoon passed quickly and when, toward its close, the professor inquired,—

FIFTEEN   "Do you see it yet?"

SIXTEEN   "No," I replied, "I am certain I do not, but I see how little I saw before."

SEVENTEEN   "That is next best," said he, earnestly, "but I won't hear you now; put away your fish and go home; perhaps you will be ready with a better answer in the morning. I will examine you before you look at the fish."

EIGHTEEN   This was disconcerting; not only must I think of my fish all night, studying, without the object before me, what this unknown but most visible feature might be, but also, without reviewing my new discoveries, I must give an exact account of them the next day. I had a bad memory; so I walked home by Charles River in a distracted state, with my two perplexities.

NINETEEN   The cordial greeting from the professor the next morning was reassuring; here was a man who seemed to be quite as anxious as I that I should see for myself what he saw.

TWENTY   "Do you perhaps mean," I asked, "that the fish has symmetrical sides with paired organs?"

TWENTY-ONE   His thoroughly pleased, "Of course, of course!" repaid the wakeful hours of the previous night. After he had discoursed most happily and enthusiastically—as he always did—upon the importance of this point, I ventured to ask what I should do next.

TWENTY-TWO   "Oh, look at your fish!" he said, and left me again to my own devices. In a little more than an hour he returned and heard my new catalogue.

TWENTY-THREE   "That is good, that is good!" he repeated, "but that is not all; go on"; and so, for three long days he placed that fish before my eyes, forbidding me to look at anything else, or to use any artificial aid. "Look, look, look," was his repeated injunction.

TWENTY-FOUR   This was the best entomological lesson I ever had— a lesson whose influence was extended to the details of every subsequent study; a legacy the professor has left to me, as he left it to many others, of inestimable value, which we could not buy, with which we cannot part.

TWENTY-FIVE   A year afterwards, some of us were amusing ourselves with chalking outlandish beasts upon the museum blackboard. We drew prancing starfishes; frogs in mortal combat; hydra-headed worms; stately crawfishes, standing on their tails, bearing aloft umbrellas; and grotesque fishes with gaping mouths and staring eyes. The professor came in shortly after, and was as amused as any at our experiments. He looked at the fishes.

TWENTY-SIX "Haemulons, every one of them," he said; "Mr. _____ drew them."

TWENTY-SEVEN True; and to this day, if I attempt a fish, I can draw nothing but Haemulons.

TWENTY-EIGHT The fourth day, a second fish of the same group was placed beside the first, and I was bidden to point out the resemblances and differences between the two; another and another followed, until the entire family lay before me, and a whole legion of jars covered the table and surrounding shelves; the odor had become a pleasant perfume: and even now, the sight of an old, six-inch, worm-eaten cork brings fragrant memories!

TWENTY-NINE The whole group of Haemulons was thus brought in review; and, whether engaged upon the dissection of the internal organs, the preparation and examination of the bony framework, or the description of the various parts, Agassiz's training in the method of observing facts and their orderly arrangement was ever accompanied by the urgent exhortation not to be content with them.

THIRTY "Facts are stupid things," he would say, "until brought into connection with some general law."

THIRTY-ONE At the end of eight months, it was almost with reluctance that I left these friends and turned to insects; but what I had gained by this outside experience has been of greater value than years of later investigation in my favorite groups.

in the laboratory with agassiz

1. From the context, which of the following definitions is best for the word _interdicted?_ (Par. 9: "I might not use a magnifying glass; instruments of all kinds were _interdicted._")
    a. ordered
    b. recommended
    c. prohibited
    d. authorized

2. The author was enrolled in the school as a student of:
    a. natural history
    b. entomology
    c. etymology
    d. icthyology

3. What is the purpose of the figure of speech in which the author says, "I

dashed the fluid over the fish as if to resuscitate it from a fainting fit"? (Par. 8)

    a. to show vividly that the fish had lost consciousness and the author was afraid that it was dead

    b. to show his panic because the fish had dried out and he was comparing the emergency with that of treating a person who has fainted

    c. to show that fish out of water must be kept wet and he made a comparison with a fainting person

    d. to show that the fish had become stiff like a fainting person, and he wanted it's normal sloppy appearance to return

4. Which of the following phrases best describes the pattern of development of this passage?

    a. gives examples of his experiences in research and comments on them

    b. gives in chronological order a description of the author's experiences in learning to see the fish

    c. gives a description of the whole experience by describing the various incidents

    d. gives a detailed and humorous account of experiences in studying a Haemulon

5. Which of the underlined words is used by the author in an emotive sense?

    a. (Par. 7: "But the example of the professor who had un-hesitatingly plunged to the bottom of the jar to produce the fish was infectious . . .")

    b. (Par. 8: ". . . and looked with anxiety for a return of a normal, sloppy appearance.")

    c. (Par. 7: ". . . I really dared not show any aversion within these sacred precincts . . .")

    d. (Par. 8: "I turned it over and around; looked it in the face —ghastly. . . .")

6. Which of the following best describes the tone of the passage in which the author tells of drawing forth "that hideous fish" and his limitations in handling it? (Par. 9)

    a. desperation

    b. resignation

    c. elation

    d. humor

7. Which of the following best describes the moral or philosophical attitude expressed in the passage, "Facts are stupid things," he would say, "until brought into connection with some general law."? (Par. 30)

    a. one should not be content with just observing facts when it does not lead you any place

    b. one should not be content with just observing facts, but should be able to arrive at some logical conclusion as a result of study of these facts

    c. facts are stupid: generalities will lead you to surer conclusions

    d. none of the above

8. Which of the following inferences seems most likely when the author writes "the odor had become a pleasant perfume; and even now, the sight of an old, six-inch, worm-eaten cork brings fragrant memories!"? (Par. 28)

   a. he had learned to enjoy the smell of the alcohol and the Haemulon

   b. the smell of the alcohol and the fish appealed to him as the smell of printer's ink appeals to the printer

   c. the author had become so accustomed to the odor that it was almost pleasing to him and the sight of a similar cork made him think of the satisfying experience he had in learning laboratory techniques

   d. the author is being very sarcastic; he hates the smell and they remind him of the gruelling experience poring over the Haemulon

9. What is the purpose of the author's description, "Those were not the days of ground glass stoppers, and elegantly shaped exhibition jars; all the old students will recall the huge, neckless glass bottles with their leaky, wax-besmeared corks, half-eaten, by insects and begrimed with cellar dust." (Par. 7)

   a. he was setting the scene to let the reader know something of the time, the feeling of antiquity of the lab, and a little of the nostalgia for a scene so antiquated, but where important research could transpire

   b. he was telling us that it was impossible to learn anything in such an antiquated and random place

   c. he was saying that the place was dirty but as suitable for research as a modern lab with its clean and attractive equipment

   d. he is implying that insects and cellar dust made icthyology a dirtier science than entomology

10. Which of the following best describes the author's intention in the passage? ("This was the best entomological lesson I ever had—a lesson whose influence was extended to the details of every subsequent study; a legacy the professor has left to me, as he left it to many others, of inestimable value, which we could not buy, with which we cannot part." (Par. 24)

   a. the author found that his lessons in observation carried over into other work and taught him something of inestimable value

   b. the author intends to show us that he not only learned the lesson, but as a legacy he received the jars of fish which were very valuable

   c. icthyology and entomology are closely related; lessons learned in one, carry over to another

   d. the author intends to convey the idea that Agassiz followed his lessons with lessons on entomology which were of inestimable value

part ix

On Vocabulary

Psychologists examining the human thought process have found in experiment after experiment that the thinking process does not involve ethereal, spiritual considerations; rather, it involves words. The implication is that one cannot expect to put into the thinking process hazy, imprecise, and nebulous words and hope to obtain a crystal clear idea. In other words, the person with an accurate and broad vocabulary will be a better thinker than a person with a meagre or inaccurate vocabulary.

A broad vocabulary is the result of years of study. One does not suddenly acquire a large vocabulary simply by memorizing a list of words in a book on vocabulary building, though this may help. A student should start early to improve his vocabulary. The best brief suggestion that I can offer is this: *be continually aware of words*. In all you hear and all you read, retain the words which appeal to you. Mentally "feel" the quality of the words for texture. Keep the words which appeal to you—words that fit your personality; then use those words.

16

comments

Vocabulary and Success

Though this selection by Johnson O'Connor dwells on the correlation of a high vocabulary to success in terms of high position and salary in the business world, I am sure that a good vocabulary is an essential ingredient for success in almost any vocational endeavor.

Given good intelligence and an ample amount of energy, the person with a good vocabulary is better able to communicate his ideas, and usually to understand the ideas of others. Often a capable but inarticulate person finds his use of the language inadequate to deal effectively in conversations with others more skilled than he in the art of self-expression. Considerable frustration is bound to result from this realization.

Vocabulary and Success

Johnson O'Connor

ONE   What is success? And how is it gained? Whether one thinks of success as financial reward, or as assured social position, or as satisfaction

From the *Atlantic Monthly,* February, 1934; reprinted in *Johnson O'Conner English Vocabulary Builder,* 1, Human Engineering Laboratory. Reprinted by permission of the author.

in able work accomplished and recognized, or as a combination of the three and something more, many factors contribute. Most of them elude our understanding and remain intangibly beyond definition. A vital force drives some persons over every obstacle. With others that great generalization, character, adds strength of a different sort. Neither may ever be restricted to a hard and fast formula; certainly, at the moment, neither can be measured. But other more concrete constituents of success have been isolated and studied in the laboratory. One of these is a large English vocabulary.

Two   An extensive knowledge of the exact meanings of English words accompanies outstanding success in this country more often than any other single characteristic which the Human Engineering Laboratory has been able to isolate and measure. . . .

Three   To measure the vocabulary of an individual the Laboratory uses a list of one hundred and fifty test words. Each is printed in a short phrase and is followed by five choices, all of which fit the phrase but only one of which is a synonym of the test word. . . .

Four   Three hundred high-school freshmen average 76 errors in the list of 150 words. Seven hundred college freshmen average 42 errors. One thousand college graduates, from a wide variety of colleges, average 27 errors, and vary from one person in a thousand who achieves a perfect score to the one who knows less than 50 of the 150 items. College professors, measured by the Laboratory, average 8 errors; major executives average 7 errors. Major executives score higher in this English vocabulary test than any other selected group with which the Laboratory has experimented.

Five   By the term *major executives* is meant all persons who, for ten years or longer, have held the position of president or vice-president in a business organization. Such a definition includes both successful and unsuccessful executives, provided only that they have survived ten years; it includes alike forceful personalities and figureheads; but it has the great advantage of excluding personal judgment from the process of selection. Major executives as thus defined average in the top ten per cent of college graduates.

Six   Although it is impossible to define success rigidly, a large vocabulary seems to be typical, not exclusively of executives, but of successful persons. It happens that in the business world successful men and women are designated by this special appellation, *executive*. The successful lawyer or doctor is marked by no such name. But if, to the best of one's ability, one selects successful persons in the professions, they also score high in vocabulary.

Seven   For one meaning of success the Century dictionary gives: "A high degree of worldly prosperity." The measured English vocabularies of executives correlate with their salaries. This does not mean that every high-vocabulary person receives a large salary, but the relation is sufficiently close to show that a large vocabulary is one element of success, and seemingly an important one.

EIGHT Furthermore, the executive level which a man or woman reaches is determined to some extent by vocabulary. In many manufacturing organizations the first step in the executive ladder is the leading hand, called sometimes the working foreman. This man is in charge of half a dozen others. He works at the bench or at a machine as they do, but is the executive of the group. The next step is the foreman, who may be in charge of as many as a hundred or more workers. He does no bench work, he is not a producer, but devotes full time to his executive duties, to the keeping of records and to the handling of the personnel. The next step in many large organizations is the department head or superintendent or manager, who ordinarily does not come in direct contact with the workers, but handles them through his foremen. The final step is the major executive or official, the vice president or president.

NINE These four executive ranks represent four degrees of success, in one sense in which that word is used. One is advanced from leading hand to foreman to manager, from manager to president. As far as the Laboratory can determine by measurements, the leading hand and the official have much the same inherent aptitudes. They differ primarily in vocabulary. Typical non-college-graduate shop foremen average, as a group, about as high as college graduates. Department heads score higher, roughly fifteen errors, and major executives the highest of all, averaging only seven errors. Whether the word *executive* refers only to the major group or is used in the broader sense to mean anyone in charge of other workers, it is still true that the executive scores higher than those under him and higher than other persons of similar age and education.

TEN An interesting sidelight on the high vocabulary scores of executives is that they were unforeseen. When a scientist expects a result and finally achieves it there is always the feeling that, regardless of the care he has taken, personal bias may have entered. Six or eight years ago the Human Engineering Laboratory tested forty major executives of the Telephone Company who had offered themselves as victims to be experimented upon in a search for executive characteristics. At the same time the Laboratory was also revising the vocabulary test, not with the notion of using it with executives, but with the hope that it might prove of value in education. One day, with no thought of the consequences, it was given to an executive, and from then on was asked for regularly because of the interest it aroused. The Laboratory paid little heed to the result until one executive refused to take the test. He had been obliged by lack of money to leave school at fourteen. With no future formal education he had worked his way to a major position. He had taken the aptitude tests without hesitation, but vocabulary seemed to him so directly the result of schooling that he knew in advance he would fail. His own words were that he had made his way without being found out and he was not willing to give himself away. But in scientific work one cannot test only those who think they will do well, and he was finally persuaded to try the vocabulary test. He made two errors where the average college graduate makes twenty-seven.

ELEVEN   Was it luck? Or was it significant of something not recognized? The Laboratory listed the vocabulary scores of one hundred executives and, parallel with them, the scores of one hundred miscellaneous college graduates. The difference between the two arrays was striking. Only nine per cent of the college graduates scored as high as the average major executive.

TWELVE   Why do large vocabularies characterize executives and possibly outstanding men and women in other fields? The final answer seems to be that words are the instruments by means of which men and women grasp the thoughts of others and with which they do much of their own thinking. They are the tools of thought.

vocabulary and success

1. From the context, which of the following definitions is best for the word *constituents?* (Par. 1: "But other more concrete *constituents* of success have been isolated and studied in the laboratory.")
   - a. electorates
   - b. components
   - c. choices
   - d. members

2. The highest scorers in a vocabulary test developed by the Human Engineering Laboratory were:
   - a. college professors
   - b. college graduates
   - c. college freshmen
   - d. major executives

3. What is the purpose of the figure of speech in which large vocabularies are compared to "tools of thought"?
   - a. it implies in order to have a large vocabulary one must use working tools called words
   - b. it means that words are instruments
   - c. it suggests that being able to converse is important in life
   - d. it implies that words are the means of thinking and of grasping the thoughts of others

4. Which of the following phrases best describes the pattern of development of this article?

a. examples of several diverse things followed by a conclusion which relates them to a moral issue

b. description of a situation leading to a conclusion about the situation

c. examples and comments on them

d. description of the parts of a whole

5. Which of the underlined words is used in an emotive sense?

a. (Par. 1: "Most of them elude our understanding and remain intangibly beyond definition.")

b. (Par. 10: ". . . who had offered themselves as victims to be experimented upon. . . .")

c. Par. 6: "Although it is impossible to define success rigidly. . . .")

d. (Par. 6: "It happens that in the business world successful men and women are designated by this special appellation, *executive.*")

6. Which of the following best describes the tone of this article?

a. logical and rhetorical

b. rhetorical and impersonal

c. descriptive and argumentative

d. logical and impersonal

7. Which of the following best describes the moral or philosophical attitude expressed in this article?

a. success in life depends on the advantages with which one is born

b. character and drive enable many people to attain great success

c. words help successful people think and grasp each others' thoughts

d. to be a success depends upon your worldly prosperity

8. Which of the following inferences seems most likely as a description of the author's attitude toward major executives?

a. he implies that all major executives have forceful personalities

b. he believes that you need an extensive vocabulary to be a successful major executive

c. he shows that major executives are successful people

d. he believes that a major executive includes anyone in charge of other workers who has a wider vocabulary than those working for him

9. What purpose is served by the author's quoting the dictionary meaning of success, "a high degree of worldly prosperity"?

a. he tries to show that all executives have a large salary

b. he proves that all high vocabulary people have correlated salaries

c. he implies that to be successful one must have money

d. he tries to show that a successful executive with a high vocabulary may have a high salary

10. Which of the following best describes the author's intention in this article?

a. he tries to prove that one of the tools of success is a high vocabulary

b. he tries to prove that wealth is important to be successful

c. he points out that a combination of three factors is important to be successful

d. he tries to show that only major executives have high vocabularies

17

comments

Comprehend Better

This selection is especially interesting because it suggests that a student can improve his (a) ability to comprehend his reading assignments, (b) academic grades, and (c) intelligence.

It may be trite when expressed, but contrary to popular opinion, reading is not a visual process alone—it is also a mental process; one must think to read. A person with a broad, accurate vocabulary has a distinct advantage. As his eyes move over words which are already familiar to him, his mind imposes accurate meaning upon the printed words, and he comprehends with accuracy. Conversely, if the eyes of another are gliding over words which are not known, or which are hazy in meaning, obviously the result will be inaccurate or hazy comprehension. Studies have shown that improvement in vocabulary results in improvement of reading.

Our experience at Cornell is similar to that of the president of an eastern engineering college whose study showed that improvement in "the accuracy of the English language" enabled the students to achieve higher academic grades.

If the findings of the psychologists are correct, that thinking is carried on by using words silently, then it follows that any increase in the quality and quantity of one's vocabulary should enable him, by just so much, to think better, and consequently to improve his level of intelligence.

Comprehend Better

One The greatest revival of interest in education that has been seen in this country in recent times is taking place today. It is concerned with one chief aim, better education. In one form or another better education is receiving hopeful attention at all levels, from the university president to the chairman of the elementary-school PTA program committee.

Two This great national anxiety over education got off the ground with Sputnik I and was in full flight by the time Sputnik II went into orbit. With the passage of time it has shown no sign of losing momentum, and gradually its shape is becoming more definable. The general consensus now is that the student simply is not doing as well as he should in any subject of study. Whether this be true or not, the pressure is certainly mounting for better trained students and improved methods of instruction.

Three As a cultural institution as well as a commercial enterprise Merriam is naturally aware of this serious problem and keenly interested in it. Constant personal contact with school and college campuses, opportunity to read the views of hundreds of correspondents, and the observations of our office staff of more than seventy editorial specialists have enabled us to analyze this situation and to come to certain conclusions about its causes. In this issue of WORD STUDY it is our intention to emphasize a major aspect of this problem as we see it and, more significantly, to suggest how we can assist you, the teacher, in your efforts to deal with it.

Four The question, stated in its simplest form, is "What can be done to improve student ability?" Our answer, stated equally concisely, is "Give the student the means to understand better what he is being taught."

Five Essential to understanding—the penetrating understanding that brings out student ability—is acurate, efficient, successful communication. In this prerequisite of all human endeavor the student and the school can admittedly do much better, but it has taken the Sputniks to make us realize this fact. Equipped with an underdeveloped vocabulary, and therefore lacking in ability to speak, read, or write his own language effectively, a student is ill prepared to face the problems of his school work and of the complex world in which he lives. What can be done?

Six Recently a well-known university conducted a survey of business and industry in an effort to determine what higher education should be doing for students that it has failed to do. The importance of vocabulary training was consistently emphasized. Ninety-eight and four-tenths per cent of the executives interviewed requested more emphasis on vocabulary study at the high school and college level and suggested greater effort toward helping students develop larger vocabularies and a higher sense of language appreciation.

SEVEN   A southwestern junior college, polling its freshman class on the assumption that students have some understanding of their own shortcomings and of their communication needs, found clear indication that more emphasis on vocabulary and spelling in the freshman English course would be of great benefit to those students.

EIGHT   The president of an eastern engineering college suggested a simple formula for the improvement of students' marks: "Those men who took pains during the freshman year to improve the accuracy of their knowledge of the English language were thereby enabled to do relatively better work in all of the sophomore courses than their fellow classmen did. Those who improved most in vocabulary averaged 3 or 4 places nearer the top of their class during the sophomore year than during their freshman year. Conversely, all the men that did not improve at all in vocabulary averaged 7.5 places nearer the bottom of the class during the sophomore year."

NINE   As an indication of the reliance placed upon vocabulary as a measure of intelligence, hundreds of corporations are today giving vocabulary tests to young men and women before employing them and before training them for key positions. The vocabulary test is also standard in determining whether older employees are capable of growing in their jobs and in discovering their special aptitudes. A word test is thus considered one of the best, if not the best, of all intelligence tests.

TEN   Vocabulary development is also the key to the reading problem. A poor reader is incapable of anything better than average achievement. Lack of comprehension in reading limits the student's environment, limits his experience in newer fields, and denies him access to the very material needed in the process of thinking. Every argument for better education is indeed an argument for better reading, since reading is the universal tool of education and an indispensable tool for intelligent life outside the school. It has been demonstrated that much of the unsatisfactory work in a "reading" subject, such as history, can be traced to inability to read. Since a poor vocabulary is one of the chief causes of poor reading, it is obvious that unfamiliar words are stumbling blocks which must be removed before the student is ready to advance toward the mastery of any subject.

ELEVEN   Studies and surveys made through the years have proved conclusively that vocabulary development is a function of college education no less than of secondary school instruction. Words are the basic building blocks which provide the foundation for both the immediate objective of a course as seen by the student and the long-range aim established by the teacher. There is increasing evidence that whoever gains a large and usable vocabulary has opened for himself many of the vistas that the sciences and the humanities offer. By contributing to the process of mental growth through assistance in vocabulary development, the English teacher is in a singularly favorable position to stimulate and inspire the student in study habits and attitudes which will serve him for life.

comprehend better

1. From the context, which of the following definitions is best for the word, *intelligence?*
   a. a successful secondary and college education
   b. word power
   c. skill in deductive reasoning
   d. innate capacity to learn

2. For what organization is this article speaking?
   a. PTA
   b. Houghton Mifflin Publishing Company
   c. Merriam Webster and Company
   d. Merriam Company

3. Why did the author use the words "basic building blocks"? (Par. 11: "Words are the basic building blocks which provide the founda- tion. . . .")
   a. to show that words have separate and distinct meanings of their own irrespective of context
   b. to show that words, like blocks, can be repositioned to build whatever a person has in mind
   c. to show that words may be just as tangible and useful as building blocks
   d. to show that words are so basic as to form the foundation for education and personal development

4. Which of the following phrases best describes the pattern of development of this article?
   a. an extended comparison of United States and Russian education
   b. seems logical, however, ends with a sales pitch to buy a dictionary
   c. statement followed by logical discussion and specific examples
   d. a series of causes and effects

5. Which of the underlined words are used by the writer in an emotive sense?
   a. (Par. 11: ". . . whoever gains a large and usable vocabu-

lary has opened for himself many of the <u>vistas</u> that the sciences and the humanities offer.")

    b. (Par. 11: "By contributing to the process of <u>mental growth</u> through assistance in vocabulary development. . . .")

    c. (Par. 10: "It is obvious that unfamiliar words are <u>stumbling</u> blocks which must be removed. . . .")

    d. (Par. 5: "Equipped with an <u>underdeveloped</u> vocabulary, and therefore lacking in ability to speak. . . .")

6. Which of the following best describes the tone of this passage?

    a. serious and optimistic
    b. impersonal and cynical
    c. serious and pessimistic
    d. humorous and figurative

7. Which of the following best describes the moral or philosophical attitude expressed in this passage?

    a. nothing has been done to help man adjust to this complex world
    b. the English language is constantly deteriorating
    c. vocabulary is a measure of intelligence
    d. vocabulary has no effect on reading habits

8. Which of the following inferences seems most likely as a description of the writer's attitudes toward word power?

    a. improving vocabulary aids daily life in the modern world
    b. vocabulary tests are unfair judges of intelligence
    c. if a man does not have a good vocabulary by the time he finishes school, he never will
    d. teaching vocabulary is the job of the secondary school teachers

9. What purpose is served by the statistical evidence?

    a. to show that research is being done, that this is an area of concern
    b. to present concrete facts showing the importance of instruction in vocabulary
    c. to show that even businessmen request further training in vocabulary
    d. all of the above

10. Which of the following best describes the writer's intention in this article?

    a. to present evidence that vocabulary is important, that it must be taught, and that people are anxious for instruction
    b. to show the presently shameful trend in vocabulary
    c. to show that a broad vocabulary only confuses and muddles the meaning
    d. to show the importance of owning a dictionary

part x

On Reading Books

The word *reading* frequently brings to mind a picture of a girl or a boy curled up in a big chair, "living" the life of Florence Nightingale, or "riding" with Marion, the Swamp Fox. Reading for pleasure is one type of reading, and it is good; but one should not live on cake alone.

The other principal type of reading which helps to provide the balanced diet is reading to learn. This type of reading is done by students—students in schools and universities, factories and mines, general offices and executive suites. To move forward, man must learn and continue learning. Now, I do not want to convey the feeling that reading to learn is drudgery—it may be, though, if you make it so.

Permit me to differentiate between these two types. The difference is purpose. The first type of reading, for pleasure, does not mean, however, that there is no learning involved in it. We all know what it is like to make serendipitous discoveries—to find valuable things not sought for. Actually, some of the most important ideas and events we know were, perhaps, discovered when we least expected them. So reading for pleasure admits learning, ranging from an incidental degree to a degree which is so great that a reversal of purpose takes place; that is, the learning motive becomes the purpose.

The other type of reading is for learning. The university "student" wants to know, has to know, and goes about his reading as a business—seriously and systematically. Some find such reading onerous. Actually, we can characterize this type as not merely reading, but as *studying*. For many, too, this type of reading may become pleasurable in varying degrees. Often the gains, intellectual or monetary, are so rewarding that a reversal takes place here too; that is, the pleasure of reading for learning becomes the purpose.

Whether you read for pleasure or profit, or just to learn, there are books for every purpose. Best of all, instead of stuporously staring at television shows or listening to the ubiquitous clichés of continued radio stories you may, as Ruskin said, talk with kings and sages.

Your life, to a degree, will be what you choose to read.

18

comments

The Best Advice I Ever Had

It is good to read about Herbert Morrison's experience, because it helps us realize the possibilities of self-instruction. We seldom think in these terms any more. Nowadays, to learn something, we must "take a course," as if the taking of a course automatically insured learning the subject matter or mastering the skill.

It was not too many years ago that some of our best educated people were self-educated people. They read because they were interested in "finding out," and as they began to "find out," they became even more interested. This cycle—one leading to the other—produced masters in a field, sometimes narrow, sometimes wide.

A man in New Haven began reading about Tibet. The more he read, the more interested he became. There are, however, some men who know more than the man from New Haven about the religions of Tibet; some know more about the topography because they have climbed mountains there, but the man from New Haven who has not been to Tibet, except through books, is the man who is continually consulted by the men in the Pentagon and the men in the State Department, because he has a full picture of the country accurately and in depth.

The man from New Haven had an advantage over Morrison, since Morrison's education had stopped with elementary school; whereas, the man from New Haven finished high school. But, think what it can mean to be a self-educated man in addition to being a college man.

The Best Advice I Ever Had

Herbert Morrison

ONE It was about ten o'clock at night on a street corner in the dimly lit Bixton section of London. In the flickering circle of light cast by a gas lamp, a tall sallow man on a soapbox harangued a small cluster of by-standers.

TWO "Learn about the most interesting subject in the world—yourself!" he shouted in a leathery voice. "Learn how to be successful! What are you good at? Let phrenology tell you!"

THREE In his hand he waved a chart of the human head colorfully divided into sections labeled "history, mathematics, memory," and so on.

FOUR A grocer's errand boy, I had no idea what phrenology was. But if the bumps on my 15-year-old noggin signified any such magnificent sounding capacities as these, I wanted to know what they were.

FIVE I stepped up and held out the thin silver sixpence which I could ill afford. The phrenologist rested his fingertips on my head and explored it, bump by bump.

SIX "That ridge above your eyes—that's originality. A fully rounded forehead—memory. Ever see a picture of Macaulay? He had a memory bump big as an egg."

SEVEN After the reading, he looked me in the eye, lowered his voice and said seriously, "You've got a good head. What do you read?"

EIGHT "Bloods, mostly," I said referring to the penny thrillers sold by news vendors. "And novelettes."

NINE "Better read trash than nothing," he said, "but you've got too good a head for that. Why not better stuff—history, biography? Read whatever you like, but develop the habit of serious reading."

TEN I was flattered that this examiner of countless heads had found something special in mine. As I walked homeward my heart beat faster. Herbert Morrison has too good a head for trash, I kept telling myself; though my education had stopped with elementary school, I was capable of serious reading.

ELEVEN Next day I took a shilling saved from my seven shillings' weekly wage and bought a copy of Macaulay's *History of England*.

Despite the fact that I had something in common with the author—my memory bump—I finished the book with a feeling of disappointment. It dealt with events too far in the past. Then I discovered Green's *Readings from English History,* a more modern work, and it fired my imagination. Through it I became aware for the first time of social problems, and I began to wonder how the conditions I saw around me in London could be improved.

TWELVE Drunkenness, for example. Why, I asked myself, did so many people drink themselves into a stupor? Who could stop them? Should we prohibit the sale of intoxicants?

THIRTEEN Ordinarily I would have wondered idly about such questions and then dismissed them. Now, thanks to the phrenologist, I knew what to do.

FOURTEEN At the library I started reading temperance pamphlets. They quickly led me to social studies of the industrial revolution and the present-day working class. Questions of bad housing, high rents, and inadequate education took on real meaning for me. I saw my fellow men in the pubs with a new understanding.

FIFTEEN The thrill of learning seized me—one of the greatest joys I had ever known. I struggled for time and a place to read. I rose in the morning an hour earlier than usual. After dressing in my heatless room above the grocery store, I wrapped myself in a blanket and read as much as I could before the grocer's wife called me to breakfast. My room was too cold to read in at night, so I went to a coffeehouse a few blocks away. There I settled myself with a book at a corner table, ordered a cup of cocoa for a half-penny and nursed it through the late evenings. That way I read Ruskin, Matthew Arnold, and Prince Kroptkin's *Fields, Factories and Workshops.*

SIXTEEN Later, when I became a telephone operator in a brewery, I read Herbert Spencer's *First Principles of Psychology* and Charles Darwin's *Origin of Species* while riding to and from work on the bus or train.

SEVENTEEN My mind teemed with ideas, and I had plenty of opportunity to test them. I spoke up at socialist meetings, union halls, and street corner discussions. I had theories as to what to do about a hundred different projects, from public health and housing, libraries and labor, to methods of sanitary inspection and drainage, refuse collection and public baths. (I felt this last issue quite personally, as I had to walk two miles for my weekly scrubbing.)

EIGHTEEN Inevitably I became a member of the political labor movement. Campaigning underlined the need for more and deeper reading, to enable me to express my thoughts and defend my conclusions. I got barrages of questions from the crowds. When I was tossed a real poser, I'd parry it as best I could and that evening "swat it up" at the library. It was amazing how often the same question would come up at the very next meeting.

NINETEEN Needless to say, all this experience was invaluable preparation for my career in the House of Commons.

TWENTY I have spent some agreeable hours listening to radio and a few watching television. I welcome the dramatic way in which much useful information is thus disseminated. But I have never heard or seen a program which revealed the value of an authoritative book. I shall always be grateful to my anonymous friend, the street corner phrenologist, for the best advice I ever had—to develop the habit of serious reading.

the best advice i ever had

1. From the context which of the following definitions is best for the word, *phrenology?* (Par. 4: "A grocer's errand boy, I had no idea what *phrenology* was.")
    a. study of the intellectual capacity
    b. study of natural temperament
    c. study of skull shapes
    d. study of the mind

2. Morrison says the most useful way of gaining information is:
    a. listening to street corner orators
    b. listening to the radio
    c. the library
    d. an authoritative book

3. What purpose is served by referring to Macaulay's memory bump? (Par. 6: "Ever see a picture of Macaulay? He had a memory bump big as an egg.")
    a. it implies all historians have large memory bumps
    b. it makes the phrenologists prediction more believable
    c. it implies people with rounded foreheads are more intelligent
    d. it implies that Morrison ought to be a future Macaulay

4. Which of the following phrases best describes the pattern of development of this passage?
    a. description of a situation leading to a conclusion about the situation
    b. examples and comments on them
    c. examples of several diverse things followed by a conclusion that relates them to a moral issue
    d. description of a whole by describing its parts

5. Which of the underlined words is used by Morrison in an emotive sense?
    a. (Par. 1: ". . . a tall sallow man on a soapbox harangued a small cluster of by-standers.")

    b. (Par. 17: "My mind <u>teemed</u> with ideas. . . .")

    c. (Par. 15: ". . . ordered a cup of cocoa for a half-penny and <u>nursed</u> it through the late evenings.")

    d. (Par. 15: "The <u>thrill</u> of learning seized me. . . .")

6. Which of the following best describes the tone of this passage?

    a. humorous and cynical
    b. humorous and rhetorical
    c. descriptive and argumentative
    d. satirical and impersonal

7. Which of the following best describes the moral or philosophical attitude expressed in this selection?

    a. a man can educate himself by reading good books
    b. a limited amount of reading can prepare you for a life in politics
    c. social weaknesses can be cured through social meetings
    d. social problems can be cured through social action

8. Which of the following inferences seems most likely to describe Morrison's attitude toward the phrenologist?

    a. a ludicrous individual
    b. an accurate predictor of the future
    c. an accurate predictor of peoples' abilities
    d. a fraud who in this case fulfilled his promise

9. What is the purpose in Morrison's saying "bloods, mostly"?

    a. it emphasizes the change brought about by the phrenologist
    b. it shows his interest in murder
    c. it points up his low level of learning
    d. it describes the popular books in London at that time

10. Which of the following best describes the author's intention in this passage?

    a. he is arguing for better health conditions
    b. he is persuading people to enter politics
    c. he is emphasizing the need to develop good reading habits
    d. he is justifying the practice of phrenology

19

comments

Can You Lose Your Taste for Reading?

There are certain classes of books which must be read at a particular time in life; otherwise they do not become a part of you. You cannot go back to pick them up. I remember the fascinating professor of literature who told our freshmen class that Omar Khayyam's *rubaiyat* must be read before the age of 21, otherwise there would be no message. As a freshmen, I was already a veteran of World War II. There was no message for me: the professor was right.

Again I was too late or too old when I read a fanciful story urged upon me by a dear friend who enjoyed it when she was ten.

It is sad to know that some fine books were missed at an age when they would have been meaningful and helpful. But saddest of all is when a taste for reading, carefully developed, is subsequently lost through disuse. This happens more frequently than one might think.

I make it a practice to ask students whether they are reading extra books. The college students always answer that they are saving up the book lists for use after they graduate and go out into the world to work. "Then," they say, "we'll have every evening free to read." No more homework, you see.

So, when I teach my special course to groups of business executives, I ask, "Gentlemen, are you reading the books that you have promised yourselves you would read once you had gotten away from your homework." They always reply, "But you don't understand, we're busier now than we ever were. We realize now that we had more time in college than most of us will ever have again. We missed the opportunity."

I then tenaciously ask, "Well, when do you expect to read?" They always answer, "When I become firmly implanted in the organization, and when my family grows up."

In my third year of working with business executives, when I had gotten to this juncture of my question-asking routine, a man of about 50, a vice-president of a large corporation stood up and said:

> Gentlemen, I have a short story to tell you. I'm pretty well set in my company. Other men do most of the work. I just supervise. My children are married and are living their own lives. As vice-president, I am privileged to six weeks vacation every summer. Well, last summer we rented a seaside cottage at Bar Harbor. I armed myself with six books that I've been wanting to read since college days—one big book per week was my plan. So with my feet on the hassock and my well-filled pipe in my mouth, I sank into a big chair to savor the books that I've waited to read for some thirty years. A half hour later I had looked through all six books and, alas! discovered I had lost my taste for reading. I've lived a life of action, a life full of striving—striving to accomplish something—and in the process I lost my taste for reading through disuse. And here I am, a major in literature, preferring to sit and watch television. I say to you younger fellows: There's no sense rushing to get somewhere when there's nothing waiting for you when you get there. If I had it to do over again, I'd take those 15 minutes, just before falling to sleep to read a bit. Perhaps if I had, I'd have seen life a bit clearer, and I'd have something for my mind to feed on now that I've gotten there.

Can You Lose Your Taste for Reading?

William James

ONE There is a passage in Darwin's short autobiography which has been often quoted, and which, for the sake of its bearing on our subject of habit, I must now quote again. Darwin says: "Up to the age of thirty or beyond it, poetry of many kinds gave me great pleasure; and even as a schoolboy I took intense delight in Shakespeare, especially in the historical plays. I have also said that pictures formerly gave me considerable, and music very great delight. But now for many years I cannot endure to read a line of poetry. I have tried lately to read Shakespeare, and

William James, *Talks to Teachers on Psychology* (New York: Holt, Rinehart & Winston, Inc., 1901). Reprinted by permission of the publisher.

found it so intolerably dull that it nauseated me. I have also almost lost my taste for pictures or music. . . . My mind seems to have become a kind of machine for grinding general laws out of large collections of facts; but why this should have caused the atrophy of that part of the brain alone, on which the higher tastes depend, I cannot conceive. . . . If I had to live my life again, I would have made a rule to read some poetry and listen to some music at least once every week; for perhaps the parts of my brain now atrophied would thus have been kept alive through use. The loss of these tastes is a loss of happiness, and may possibly be injurious to the intellect, and more probably to the moral character, by enfeebling the emotional part of our nature."

Two   We all intend when young to be all that may become a man, before the destroyer cuts us down. We wish and expect to enjoy poetry always, to grow more and more intelligent about pictures and music, to keep in touch with spiritual and religious ideas, and even not to let the greater philosophic thoughts of our time develop quite beyond our view. We mean all this in youth, I say; and yet in how many middle-aged men and women is such an honest and sanguine expectation fulfilled? Surely, in comparatively few; and the laws of habit show us why. Some interest in each of these things arises in everybody at the proper age; but, if not persistently fed with the appropriate matter, instead of growing into a powerful and necessary habit, it atrophies and dies, choked by the rival interests to which the daily food is given. We make ourselves into Darwins in this negative respect by persistently ignoring the essential practical conditions of our case. We say abstractly: "I mean to enjoy poetry, and to absorb a lot of it, of course. I fully intend to keep up my love of music, to read the books that shall give new turns to the thought of my time, to keep my higher spiritual side alive, etc." But we do not attack these things concretely, and we do not begin *today*. We forget that every good that is worth possessing must be paid for in strokes of daily effort. We postpone and postpone, until those smiling possibilities are dead. Whereas ten minutes a day of poetry, of spiritual reading or meditation, and an hour or two a week at music, pictures, or philosophy, provided we began *now* and suffered no remission, would infallibly give us in due time the fulness of all we desire. By neglecting the necessary concrete labor, by sparing ourselves the little daily tax, we are postively digging the graves of our higher possibilities.

can you lose your taste for reading?

1.   From the text which of the following definitions is best for *atrophy*? (Par. 1: ". . . but why this should have caused the *atrophy* of that part of the brain alone. . . .")

    a. ravaging
    b. squandering
    c. wasting away
    d. devastation

2. How much time did Darwin feel one should spend listening to music?
    a. an hour a day
    b. an hour a week
    c. ten minutes a day
    d. at least once a week

3. What is the purpose of the words "to which the daily food is given"? (Par. 2)
    a. it underlines the concept of habit
    b. it implies the necessity of earning a living
    c. it implies that giving thought to spiritual ideas is as necessary as daily food
    d. it is used to give a light tone to the selection

4. Which of the following best describes the pattern of development of this passage?
    a. description of a whole by describing its parts
    b. examples and comments on them
    c. description of an event followed by a conclusion which relates it to a moral
    d. example followed by insight based on the example

5. Which of the underlined words is used by James in an emotive sense?
    a. (Par. 1: "But now for many years I cannot endure to read a line of poetry.")
    b. (Par. 1: ". . . and found it so intolerably dull that it nauseated me.")
    c. (Par. 1: "The loss of these tastes is a loss of happiness. . . .")
    d. (Par. 1: ". . . by enfeebling the emotional part of our nature.")

6. Which of the following best describes the tone of this passage?
    a. playful and humorous
    b. condescending and informal
    c. personal and intellectually appealing
    d. impersonal and ironic

7. Which of the following best describes the moral or philosophical attitude expressed by James?
    a. all people need the arts to provide balance in their lives
    b. reading is a means of personal enrichment
    c. even a good habit must first be established
    d. age brings atrophying of parts of the brain

8. Which of the following inferences describes James's feeling about youth?
    a. a time when it is possible to foretell what a person will become
    b. a period of many awakening interests
    c. a time when people appreciate the arts
    d. a time when people develop good habits

9. What is the purpose of James's quoting Darwin?

    a. as an introduction
    b. he wishes to make the same point
    c. he wants to lend strength to his point by quoting from a
    well known source
    d. he wishes to use the quotation as a basis for his point

10. Which of the following best describes the author's intention in this
    selection?

    a. an understanding of the arts is necessary for an educated
    man
    b. active participation in the arts is necessary for the total
    fulfillment of man
    c. the arts are more appreciated by the young than by the
    middle aged
    d. the arts are more important than the sciences

20

comments

Students must be wary not to equate the passing of examinations with getting an education. Missing a chance at an education is just as easy in engineering as it is in literature.

The engineer can memorize formulas by rote sufficiently well to make correct calculations on examinations, and the student of literature can scribble pages of verbiage to cover the questions asked. Both students can pass an exam but not know their subject.

"Well, how should one study his books to become fully educated?" one may ask. The best way to learn through books is by asking questions continually. The engineer may ask, "What really makes this formula work? Why is it true? Are there exceptions? How does this bit of information fit in with what I already know?"

The student of literature may ask, "What is the author's controlling idea? What do the various parts contribute to defining the subject? What are the key words? What are the author's basic arguments and assumptions?"

Using the questioning approach, both students cease to be spectators; instead, they become players—participants. The concepts no longer belong to the page alone. The concepts having been processed through both brain and being, are now truly a part of each student.

To get back to Mortimer Adler, he says, in effect, "Don't fool yourselves into thinking that because you have read all *about* a book in secondary sources that you *know* the book. There is only one true way to *know* a book and that is through the book itself."

How to Read a Book

Mortimer J. Adler

I did not discover I could not read until after I had left college. I found it out only after I tried to teach others how to read. Most parents have probably made a similar discovery by trying to teach their youngsters. Paradoxically, as a result, the parents usually learn more about reading than their children. The reason is simple. They have to be more active about the business. Anyone who teaches anything has to.

To get back to my story. So far as the registrar's records were concerned, I was one of the satisfactory students in my day at Columbia. We passed courses with creditable marks. The game was easy enough, once you caught on to the tricks. If anyone had told us then that we did not know much or could not read very well, we would have been shocked. We were sure we could listen to lectures and read the books assigned in such a way that we could answer examination questions neatly. That was the proof of our ability.

Some of us took one course which increased our self-satisfaction enormously. It had just been started by John Erskine. It ran for two years, was called General Honors, and was open to a select group of juniors and seniors. It consisted of nothing but "reading" the great books, from the Greek classics through the Latin and medieval masterpieces right down to the best books of yesterday, William James, Einstein, and Freud. The books were in all fields: they were histories and books of science or philosophy, dramatic poetry and novels. We read a book a week, some sixty in two years, and we discussed them with our teachers one night a week in informal, seminar fashion.

That course had two effects on me. For one thing, it made me think I had struck educational gold for the first time. Here was real stuff, handled in a real way, compared to the textbook and lecture courses that merely made demands on one's memory. But the trouble was I not only thought I had struck gold; I also thought that I owned the mine. Here were the great books. I knew how to read. The world was my oyster.

If, after graduation, I had gone into business or medicine or law, I would probably still be harboring the conceit that I knew how to read and was well read beyond the ordinary. Fortunately, something woke

Mortimer J. Adler, *How to Read a Book* (New York: Simon and Schuster, Inc., 1940), pp. 6–11. Copyright 1940 by Mortimer J. Adler. Reprinted by permission of Simon and Schuster, Inc.

me from this dream. For every illusion that the classroom can nourish, there is a school of hard knocks to destroy it. A few years of practice awaken the lawyer and the doctor. Business or newspaper work disillusions the boy who thought he was a trader or a reporter when he finished the school of commerce or journalism. Well, I thought I was liberally educated, that I knew how to read, and had read a lot. The cure for that was teaching, and the punishment that precisely fitted my crime was having to teach, the year after I graduated, in this very Honors course which had so inflated me.

As a student I had read all the books I was now going to teach but, being very young and conscientious, I decided to read them again—you know, just to brush up each week for class. To my growing amazement, week after week, I discovered that the books were almost brand new to me. I seemed to be reading them for the first time, these books which I thought I had "mastered" thoroughly.

As time went on, I found out not only that I did not know very much about any of these books, but also that I did not know how to read them very well. To make up for my ignorance and incompetence I did what any young teacher might do who was afraid of both his students and his job. I used secondary sources, encyclopedias, commentaries, all sorts of books about books about these books. In that way, I thought, I would appear to know more than the students. They wouldn't be able to tell that my questions or points did not come from my better reading of the book they too were working on.

Fortunately for me I was found out, or else I might have been satisfied with getting by as a teacher just as I had got by as a student. If I had succeeded in fooling others, I might soon have deceived myself as well. My first good fortune was in having as a colleague in this teaching Mark Van Doren, the poet. He led off in the discussion of poetry, as I was supposed to do in the case of history, science, and philosophy. He was several years my senior, probably more honest than I, certainly a better reader. Forced to compare my performance with his, I simply could not fool myself. I had not found out what the books contained by reading them, but by reading *about* them.

My questions about a book were of the sort anyone could ask or answer without having read the book—anyone who had had recourse to the discussions which a hundred secondary sources provide for those who cannot or do not want to read. In contrast, his questions seemed to arise from the pages of the book itself. He actually seemed to have some intimacy with the author. Each book was a large world, infinitely rich for exploration, and woe to the student who answered questions as if, instead of traveling therein, he had been listening to a travelogue. The contrast was too plain, and too much for me. I was not allowed to forget that *I did not know how to read.*

My second good fortune lay in the particular group of students who formed that first class. They were not long in catching on to me. They knew how to use the encyclopedia, or a commentary, or the editor's introduction which usually graces the publication of a classic, just as well as I did. One of them, who has since achieved fame as a critic, was particularly obstreperous. He took what seemed to me endless delight in discussing the various theories about the book, which could be obtained from secondary sources, always to show me and the rest of the class that the book itself still remained to be discussed. I do not mean that he or the other students could really read the book better than I, or had done so. Clearly none of us, with the exception of Mr. Van Doren, was doing the job of reading.

After the first year of teaching, I had few illusions left about my literacy. Since then, I have been teaching students how to read books, six years at Columbia with Mark Van Doren and for the last ten years at the University of Chicago with President Robert M. Hutchins. In the course of years, I think I have gradually learned to read a little better. There is no longer any danger of self-deception, of supposing that I have become expert. Why? Because reading the same books year after year, I discover each time what I found out the first year I began to teach: the book I am rereading is almost new to me. For a while, each time I reread it I thought, naturally enough, that I had mastered it, that I had really read it well at last, only to have the next reading show up my inadequacies and misinterpretations. After this happens several times, even the dullest of us is likely to learn that perfect reading lies at the end of the rainbow. Although practice makes perfect, in this art of reading as in any other, the long run needed to prove the maxim is longer than the allotted span.

I am torn between two impulses. I certainly want to encourage you to undertake this business of learning to read, but I do not want to fool you by saying that it is quite easy or that it can be done in a short time. I am sure you do not want to be fooled. As in the case of every other skill, learning to read well presents difficulties to be overcome by effort and time. Anyone who undertakes anything is prepared for that, I think, and knows that the achievement seldom exceeds the effort. After all, it takes time and trouble to grow up from the cradle, to make a fortune, raise a family, or gain the wisdom that some old men have. Why should it not take time and trouble to learn to read and to read what is worth reading?

Of course, it would not take so long if we got started when we were in school. Unfortunately, almost the opposite happens: *one gets stopped. . . .* Here I wish only to record this fact about our schools, a fact which concerns us all, because in large part they have made us what we are today—people who cannot read well enough to enjoy reading for profit or to profit by reading for enjoyment.

But education does not stop with schooling, nor does the responsibility for the ultimate educational fate of each of us rest entirely on the school system. Everyone can and must decide for himself whether he is satisfied with the education he got, or is now getting if he is still in school. If he is not satisfied, it is up to him to do something about it. With schools as they are, more schooling is hardly the remedy. One way out—perhaps the only one available to most people—is to learn to read better, and then, by reading better, to learn more of what can be learned through reading.

how to read a book

1. From the context, which of the following definitions is best for the word, *obstreperous*? (Par. 10: "One of them, who has since achieved fame as a critic, was particularly *obstreperous*.")
    a. annoying
    b. cantankerous
    c. stubborn
    d. disturbing

2. The author mentions his good fortune in having a colleague who knew how to read. What was his second good fortune?
    a. by continually trying one's best, the goal of perfection in reading will eventually be reached
    b. going through the school of "hard knocks"
    c. the students in his first class
    d. by continually trying one's best, one continues to improve and draws nearer and nearer to the goal of perfect reading

3. What is the purpose of the figure of speech in the sentence, ". . . perfect reading lies at the end of the rainbow."?
    a. perfect reading is as priceless as the "pot of gold"
    b. one should seek to reach for horizons in his reading
    c. like a rainbow, perfect reading is the subtle blending of many hues
    d. none of these

4. Which of the following best describes the pattern of development in this essay?
    a. an illustrated problem and conclusion
    b. an introduction, discussion, and conclusion
    c. an argument leading to a conclusion
    d. two main themes, with illustrations

5. Which of the following words is used by the author in an emotive sense?
    a. incompetence   (Par. 7: "To make up for my ignorance and *incompetence*, I did what any young teacher might do. . . .")

b. travelogue   (Par. 9: ". . . and woe to the student who answered questions as if, instead of traveling therein, he had been listening to a *travelogue*.")

c. illusions   (Par. 11: "After the first year of teaching, I had few *illusions* left about my literacy.")

d. intimacy   (Par. 9: "He actually seemed to have some *intimacy* with the author.")

6. Which of the following best describes the tone of this passage?
    - **a.** serious and moralistic
    - **b.** descriptive and cynical
    - **c.** moralistic and cynical
    - **d.** serious and descriptive

7. Which of the following best describes the moral or philosophical attitude expressed in this paper?
    - **a.** our school systems actually discourage students from learning to read well
    - **b.** college students read to pass examinations, and stop reading when school is over
    - **c.** most people who think they know how to read are deceiving themselves
    - **d.** learning to read well cannot come without constant practice and intensive reading

8. The author states, "We were sure we could listen to lectures and read books assigned in such a way that we could answer examination questions neatly." Based on this, which of the following inferences seems most likely as a statement of the author's attitude toward his college education?
    - **a.** he was overconfident of his ability and accomplishments
    - **b.** he had equated good exam results with good learning
    - **c.** he had been deceived about the meaning of learning
    - **d.** he had learned nothing more than a good technique

9. What purpose is served by the author's contrast of himself and his colleague in teaching the General Honors course?
    - **a.** it shows that his colleague knew how to "grasp" the essence of a book
    - **b.** the author uses his colleague as evidence that people can read very well
    - **c.** it shows that some people are born with a knack for teaching
    - **d.** it lends credence to the author's claim that he did not know how to read

10. Which of the following best describes the author's intention in this selection?
    - **a.** to break down the reader's illusion that he can read well
    - **b.** to identify with poor readers and urge them on to increased reading
    - **c.** to give the reader practical suggestions on how to read
    - **d.** to remind us that there is no substitute for actual reading

Appendix

I. Meaning of Words in Context

In reading for understanding you must pause long enough to look up all words that you do not know. Unless you do, you run the risk of imposing upon a passage your meaning which may not be the meaning intended by the author. Here is what Professor Hayakawa [1] says about words in context:

The "One Word, One Meaning" Fallacy

Everyone, of course, who has ever given any thought to the meaning of words has noticed that they are always shifting and changing in meaning. Usually, people regard this as a misfortune, because it "leads to sloppy thinking" and "mental confusion." To remedy this condition, they are likely to suggest that we should all agree on "one meaning" for each word and use it only with that meaning. Thereupon it will occur to them that we simply cannot make people agree in this way, even if we could set up an ironclad dictatorship under a committee of lexicographers who could place censors in every newspaper office and microphones in every home. The situation, therefore, appears hopeless.

Such an impasse is avoided when we start with a new premise altogether—one of the premises upon which modern linguistic thought is based: namely, *that no word ever has exactly the same meaning twice*. The extent to which this premise fits the facts can be demonstrated in a number of ways. . . . If we accept the proposition that the contexts of an utterance determine its meaning, it becomes apparent that since no two contexts are ever *exactly* the same, no two meanings can ever be exactly the same. How can we "fix the meaning" even for as common an expression as "to believe in" when it can be used in such sentences as the following:

[1] From S. I. Hayakawa, *Language in Thought and Action,* Revised Edition (New York: Harcourt, Brace & World, Inc., 1964). © 1964 by Harcourt, Brace & World, Inc., and reprinted with their permission.

I believe in you (I have confidence in you).

I believe in democracy (I accept the principles implied by the term democracy).

I believe in Santa Claus (It is my opinion that Santa Claus exists). . . .

To insist dogmatically that we know what a word means *in advance of its utterance* is nonsense. All we can know in advance is *approximately* what it will mean. After the utterance, we interpret what has been said in the light of both verbal and physical contexts, and act according to our interpretation. . . .

Ignoring Contexts

It is clear, then, that the ignoring of contexts in any act of interpretation is at best a stupid practice. At its worst, it can be a vicious practice. A common example is the sensational newspaper story in which a few words by a public personage are torn out of their context and made the basis of a completely misleading account. There is the incident of a Veterans Day speaker, a university teacher, who declared before a high school assembly that the Gettysburg Address was "a powerful piece of propaganda." The context clearly revealed that "propaganda" was being used, not according to its popular meaning, but rather, as the speaker himself stated, to mean "explaining the moral purposes of a war." The context also revealed that the speaker was a great admirer of Lincoln. However, the local newspaper, ignoring the context, presented the account in such a way as to suggest that the speaker had called Lincoln a liar. On this basis, the newspaper began a campaign against the instructor. The speaker remonstrated with the editor of the newspaper, who replied, in effect, "I don't care what else you said. You said the Gettysburg Address was propaganda, didn't you?" This appeared to the editor complete proof that Lincoln had been maligned and that the speaker deserved to be discharged from his position at the university. . . .

The Interaction of Words

All this is not to say, however, that the reader might just as well throw away his dictionary, simply because contexts are so important. Any word in a sentence—any sentence in a paragraph, any paragraph in a larger unit—whose meaning is revealed by its context, is itself part of the context of the rest of the text. To look up a word in a dictionary therefore, frequently explains not only the word itself, but the rest of the sentence, paragraph, conversation, or essay in which it is found. All words within a given context interact upon one another.

Realizing, then, that a dictionary is a historical work, we

should understand the dictionary thus: "The word *mother* has most frequently been used in the past among English-speaking people to indicate a female parent." From this we can safely infer, "If that is how it has been used, that is what it *probably* means in the sentence I am trying to understand." This is what we normally do, of course; after we look up a word in the dictionary, we reexamine the context to see if the definition fits. If the context reads, "Mother began to form in the bottle," one may have to look at the dictionary more carefully.

A dictionary definition, therefore, is an invaluable guide to interpretation. Words do not have a single, "correct meaning"; they apply to *groups* of similar situations, which might be called *areas of meaning*. It is for defining these areas of meaning that a dictionary is useful. In each use of any word, we examine the particular context and the extensional events denoted (if possible) to discover the *point* intended within the area of meaning.

There is no quick, easy way to remedy a weak vocabulary, but a fast start can be made by wide and varied reading and by consulting a dictionary when you do not know a word. The effort of looking up words will help associate the word in your mind for the next time you encounter it.

II.   Understanding Statements Explicitly Made

When you are asked about an explicit statement in a passage, your instructor may be merely checking to see whether you have read the material carefully, if at all. Such questions should not be difficult to answer, for by definition an explicit statement is "clearly stated, distinctly expressed, definite." All that you need do is read the passage. For example, notice how explicit are the statements in the following passage.

Tired, weary, and disappointed, the seven men slowly trudged down the snowy mountain side—the story was revealed in their grim faces.

"Seven men" is very explicit. It is also explicit that they were descending the mountain. Furthermore, it is directly stated that they were tired, weary, and disappointed. In this sentence, you come directly upon this information.

Let us look at another example containing statements explicitly made. At the end of this excerpt, three questions will be asked. Answer them before reading the next paragraph, which contains the correct answers.

There are several kinds of stories, but only one difficult kind —the humorous. I will talk mainly about that one. The humorous story is American, the comic story is English, the witty story is French. The humorous story depends for its effect upon the *manner* of the telling; the comic story and the witty story upon the *matter*.[1]

Question 1: Which of the following is the only difficult kind of story? (a) the comic story; (b) the humorous story; (c) the witty story.

Question 2: With which of the following would one associate a witty story? (a) America; (b) England; (c) France.

Question 3: In which of the following is the manner of telling a story the most important? (a) in the humorous story; (b) in the witty story; (c) in a comic story.

The answers are b, c, a.

A test of an explicit question is your ability to answer it by pointing to the author's words contained in the text. You should be aware, however, that not all questions dealing with this category (understanding statements explicitly made) are easy. A good instructor is concerned with accomplishing more than a check on whether or not you have read the assignment.

He may want to check on some reading skills of a higher order, yet remain within the bounds of this category. He may want to check on your ability to perceive the significance of subtle details; to see differences among them; and to choose the ones which, in your judgment, contribute, for example, the most to the building of a character, a theme, or some other purpose which the author may have intended.

The purpose of this category of questions is to emphasize the importance of looking at the author's words intensely to get at his real meaning. This skill of "reading the lines" to get at the explicit meaning is a necessary prelude to "reading between the lines," to get at his implicit meaning. There are still, of course, additional reading skills which must be used for getting at the author's total meaning.

III. Interpreting Allusions and Figures of Speech

A figure of speech is an expression using words in an imaginative and nonliteral sense for the purpose of intensifying statements—making writing more concrete and more alive—thus, more interesting. For example,

---

[1] Samuel L. Clemens, *How to Tell a Story* (Hartford, Conn.: The American Publishing Company, 1900), p. 7.

a nonfigurative statement such as "The fewer words a person uses, the more quickly his meaning will be understood," can be expressed in a much more memorable way by the following figure of speech: ". . . meaning is an arrow that reaches its mark when least encumbered with feathers."

The two most popular figures of speech, both of which involve comparisons, are the *simile* and the *metaphor*. A simile is an explicit comparison between two things which differ in kind or quality and is usually introduced by "like" or "as." For example: (a) He held on tenaciously, like a bulldog. (b) She moved quietly and softly as a feather.

Stating that "Congress is like a state legislature," however, is not a simile because the two things being compared do not differ from each other either in kind or quality. It is instead simply a statement of fact.

Whereas the simile says specifically that one thing is like another (using the words "like" or "as"), the metaphor merely implies the likeness. This is often done by asserting that one thing *is* another, as when Herbert Read said, above, ". . . meaning *is* an arrow that reaches its mark when least encumbered with feathers." (Emphasis added.) Other examples of metaphors are: His mind is a vise; his memory a filing cabinet.

Two other effective and widely used figures of speech are *hyperbole* (extreme exaggeration) and *meiosis* (understatement). (1) *Hyperbole* is a deliberate overstatement or fanciful exaggeration which has as its purpose emphasis rather than deception. For example: (a) The waves were mountains high. (b) I'm dead tired. (c) A thousand thanks. (d) I'm thrilled to pieces. In using the hyperbole, however, it should be remembered that although it serves to make certain points more vivid, indiscriminate use of exaggeration can be weakening and, therefore, should be avoided. (2) Just as things can be exaggerated, so can they also be understated. This particular figure of speech, *meiosis*, often takes the form of irony by implying something markedly different, sometimes even the opposite, from what is actually said. It can also be used, however, simply to state an idea in negative terms or in less strong words than would normally be expected—as in the remark, "Picasso is not a bad painter."

There is yet another important literary term which must be understood if intelligent reading is to take place. The term, *allusion*, is an indirect reference in an essay or other writing to a person, place, or event which is generally familiar to most readers and which stands for pages or even volumes of additional meaning. For example, "Trent's love of praise is his Achilles heel," refers to a famous Greek warrior, Achilles, who took part in the Trojan War.

When Achilles was born, his mother made him invulnerable to death by dipping him into the River Styx. One part of his body that the water did not touch was his heel by which his mother held him; thus the heel was his only vulnerable spot. As fate would have it, during a battle with the Trojans, he was killed when an arrow shot by Paris struck his heel.

The remark, "Trent's love of praise is his Achilles heel" means therefore, that Trent is a strong person, practically invulnerable, except for one weakness: his love of praise which is *his* Achilles heel.

Whenever you encounter an allusion which is not familiar to you, look it up in a reference book, for often the full meaning of a passage will depend on your knowing the idea, person, or event alluded to.

One of the surest ways to build up a good background is to purchase a book on Greek and Roman mythology, and every evening take time to read just one myth; then, during the following day, recall and reflect on that myth. Reflecting on the myth during your spare moments will fix the myth in your memory where it will be ready for use in reading, writing, and reverie.

IV.   Recognizing Patterns of Development

Being able to answer correctly the question, "Which of the following phrases best describes the pattern of development of this selection?" depends largely upon two skills of reading: first, a general skill—reading closely to comprehend the author's ideas; and second, a specific skill—detecting how the author has arranged his ideas.

Though these two skills of reading are listed separately, you should not assume that the act of reading is thus fragmented, or that one skill has priority over another. Actually, in most good writing, the ideas and the arrangement are interwoven. Though they are interwoven, the ideas and the structure are, nevertheless, just as discernible as are the bones and the flesh of the human body. Your job as a reader is to perceive the author's arrangement of ideas so that you can arrive at his full meaning.

To help you perceive the author's pattern of organization during the act of reading, it would be helpful to know in advance some of the more commonly used patterns. Presenting some of these patterns is the purpose of this exposition.

As order appears inherent in so much of man's activity and thinking, it is only natural that a *Chronological Pattern* of writing should have developed, based upon events or experiences occurring in a time sequence. This pattern is often used in relating the events of a narrative, for example, in writing the story of Napoleon's defeat or in recounting the day's adventures. It may also be used in describing a process such as the proper way to apply make-up or the stages of the development of a frog.

Time, however, is not the only dimension about which one can organize or order his thoughts. Space can also be used in this capacity and is especially effective when one wishes to describe objects in expository writing. Whenever authors describe cities from outskirts to center, ships from bow to stern, or murals from right to left, they are making use of the *Spatial Pattern* of organization.

A third method of arranging one's thoughts is in order of *Increasing Complexity,* beginning with the simple or familiar and proceeding to the more complex or unfamiliar. Discussing present day orchestral wind instruments by beginning with the toy whistle would be an example of this particular pattern.

Comparison and Contrast provides yet another method of presenting one's ideas. It involves discussing all the features of one idea or situation, then all the features of another, and ending by drawing a conclusion about the two. Both of the following topics lend themselves to this pattern of development: "Mississippi and the Congo," and "Girls' College *v.* Co-ed Institutions."

When a passage begins with a general statement or impression followed by specific examples, details, or reasons, the author is most likely using the *Support Pattern.* If he addresses himself to a specific problem, emphasizing its causes and suggesting several solutions, he is making use of the *Problem-Causes-Solution Pattern.* If, on the other hand, he stresses the effects of a problem and outlines a definite course of action, he is illustrating the *Problem-Effect-Solution Pattern.*

Many passages, however, do not fit neatly into one of these categories, and the reader must construct his own definition of a pattern, just as the writer or author, as artist, often constructs his own unique design. In other words, one should not try to force a particular passage into one of the categories with which one happens to be familiar.

One way to discover pattern is to see whether a passage can be divided into parts and to decide what function these parts serve and how they relate to the whole. Perhaps attempting an outline of the passage would be helpful. Is there any kind of introduction or conclusion? Does the author begin in the middle of his subject and then slowly fit the pieces of the passage together, depending on his reader's ability to grasp the whole? Are several ideas presented, and if so how are they related? Does the author depend largely on metaphor or allegory to convey his idea? Often, one must look for some key sentence or idea and then determine how it is developed.

The writer must shape his ideas upon some sort of framework. Often he attempts to hide or blur this framework so that his idea appears more convincing to the casual reader who doesn't detect the method used to make him accept an idea or attitude. By examining each sentence or paragraph in relation to the one which precedes or follows it, by asking questions similar to the ones above, and by seeking to define the particular relationship of the parts to each other and to the whole, the careful reader is at least on his way to discovering a pattern of development.

Remember! The author who writes without an organizational plan is like a woman who makes a coat without a pattern. Invariably, the better the pattern, the better the product, be it coat or composition.

V.   Recognizing the Use of Emotive Words

Once we have determined an author's general subject matter, an effective way to detect the position he takes in regard to his subject is to analyze his language. The way an author uses his words within certain contexts reveals his feelings and attitudes. Such words are called emotive or loaded words. They are related to words used in a connotative sense; they are figurative rather than literal; they imply or suggest meanings beyond themselves.

Emotive words, in particular, have emotional overtones suggesting either approval or disapproval of persons, things, or ideas. Thus, emotive language in general and emotive words in particular, have a somewhat more specific function than words used in a connotative sense. While an author's general interpretation of thoughts on a subject may be seen by his use of connotative words, a greater insight into the feelings which combine to form his point of view may be discovered by his use of emotive words.

To provide an opportunity for additional insights into the topic of emotive or loaded language, the following excerpt from a book by Thouless is reprinted.[1]

> When we use a word in speech and writing, its most obvious purpose is to point to some thing or relation or property. This is the word's "meaning." We see a small four-footed animal on the road and call it a "dog," indicating that it is a member of the class of four-footed animals we call dogs. The word "dog" as we have

[1] Robert H. Thouless, *How to Think Straight* (New York: Simon and Schuster, Inc., 1939). Copyright 1939 by Simon and Schuster, Inc., and reprinted with their permission.

used it there has a plain, straightforward, "objective" meaning. We have in no way gone beyond the requirements of exact scientific description.

Let us suppose also that one grandparent of the dog was a collie, another was an Irish terrier, another a fox terrier, and the fourth a bulldog. We can express these facts equally scientifically and objectively by saying that he is a dog of mixed breed. Still we have in no way gone beyond the requirements of exact scientific description.

Suppose, however, that we had called that same animal a "mongrel." The matter is more complicated. We have used a word which objectively means the same as "dog of mixed breed," but which also arouses in our hearers an emotional attitude of disapproval toward that particular dog. A word, therefore, cannot only indicate an object, but can also suggest an emotional attitude toward it. Such suggestions of an emotional attitude do go beyond exact and scientific discussion because our approvals and disapprovals are individual—they belong to ourselves and not to the objects we approve or disapprove of. An animal which to the mind of its master is a faithful and noble dog of mixed ancestry may be a "mongrel" to his neighbor whose chickens are chased by it.

Once we are on the lookout for this difference between "objective" and "emotional" meanings, we shall notice that words which carry more or less strong suggestions of emotional attitudes are very common and are ordinarily used in the discussion of such controversial questions as those of politics, morals, and religion. This is one reason why such controversies cannot yet be settled.

There is a well-known saying that the word "firm" can be declined as follows: I am *firm,* thou art *obstinate,* he is *pigheaded.* That is a simple illustration of what is meant. "Firm," "obstinate," and "pigheaded" all have the same objective meaning—that is, following one's own course of action and refusing to be influenced by other people's opinions. They have, however, different emotional meanings: "firm" has an emotional meaning of strong approval, "obstinate" of mild disapproval, "pigheaded" of strong disapproval.

Since the category of questions titled "Recognizing Use of Emotive Words" is an especially difficult one for most students, I am including, as additional instruction, the ideas which Professor S. I. Hayakawa,[2] a noted linguist, has on this topic. Please notice, however, that Professor Hayakawa believes that the word "emotive" may imply misleading distinctions between the "emotional appeals" and "intellectual appeals" of language; therefore, in the following excerpt you will find that he uses the word "affective" in place of the word "emotive."

---

[2] S. I. Hayakawa, *Language in Thought and Action* (New York: Harcourt, Brace & World, Inc., 1964). Used by permission of publisher.

Informative Connotations

The informative connotations of a word are its socially agreed upon, "impersonal" meanings, *insofar as meanings can be given at all by additional words.* For example, if we talk about a "pig," we cannot give the extensional meaning of the word unless there happens to be an actual pig for us to point to. But we can give its informative connotations: "pig" for English-speaking people means "domesticated mammalian quadruped of the kind generally raised by farmers to be made into pork, bacon, ham, lard. . . ."

Affective Connotations

The affective connotations of a word, on the other hand, are the aura of personal feelings it arouses, as, for example, "pig": "Ugh! Dirty, evil-smelling creatures, wallowing in filthy sties," and so on. While there is no necessary agreement about these feelings—some people like pigs and others don't—it is the existence of these feelings that enables us to use words, under certain circumstances, *for their affective connotations alone,* without regard to their informative connotations. That is to say, when we are strongly moved, we express our feelings by uttering words with the affective connotations appropriate to our feelings, without paying any attention to the informative connotations they may have. We angrily call people "rats," "wolves," "old bears," "skunks," or lovingly call them "honey," "sugar," "duck," and "sweetie pie." Indeed, all verbal expressions of feeling make use to some extent of the affective connotations of words.

All words have, according to the uses to which they are put, some affective character. There are many words that exist more for their affective value than for their informative value; for example, we can refer to "that man" as "that gentleman," "that individual," "that person," "that gent," "that guy," "that hombre," "that bird," or "that bozo"—and while the person referred to may be the same in all these cases, each of these terms reveals a difference in our feelings toward him. Dealers in knicknacks frequently write "Gyfte Shoppe" over the door, hoping that such a spelling carries, even if their merchandise does not, the flavor of antiquity. Affective connotations suggestive of England and Scotland are often sought in the choice of brand names for men's suits and overcoats: "Glenmoor," "Regent Park," "Bond Street." Sellers of perfume choose names for their products that suggest France—"Mon Désir," "Indiscret," "Evening in Paris"—and expensive brands always come in "flacons," never in bottles.

Since an author's feelings can best be determined by his choice of words, the unequivocal advice given by Ruskin in his essay "Of Kings' Treasuries" takes on deeper meaning. He said, "You must get the habit of looking intensely at words, and assuring yourself of their meaning, syllable by syllable—nay, letter by letter."

VI. Recognizing the Author's Tone

To identify the author's tone in a passage is just the same as identifying the author's attitude toward his subject and toward his readers. The author indicates this tone or attitude in his work by his choice and arrangement of words. By treating his material in a particular manner, an author has the power to say to his reader: "Can you see this delights me," or "I am now condemning this topic," or "I wish to be respectful and reverent."

In exactly the same way, a speaker can indicate his attitude toward his subject and his listener by making the tone of his voice sad, happy, or indifferent. In a group conversation, it is often easy to tell who favors a subject and who dislikes a subject by the attitude or tone of voice used.

Tone is very important in both the written and the spoken word. Without careful consideration of tone, the author could not communicate his way of thinking and his way of feeling toward an experience. The tone or expression used serves to point out the writer's relation to the reader in view of what is being said and their joint feelings about it. We say an author is good if he has the talent to set and sustain a certain tone without breaking it, or if he has the ability to shift effectively from one tone to another.

Tone, however, must not be confused with the terms of atmosphere or mood which are used to describe the world in which the characters move. The mood or atmosphere of a passage or novel may be gruesome and horrible, but the author's tone or attitude toward this condition he has created may be one of sympathy, compassion, or bewilderment.

The attitude or tone of an author can have a far-reaching effect on the value of a work. A writer can turn a dull and overworked topic into a something fresh and startling merely by reacting to it in a different tone. For instance, instead of crying over the concept of death, many authors laugh at it or defy it. Or an author can purposefully convey a serious message or even induce the reader to action by the tone he uses. An author can be so logical and descriptive that just by his tone he may convince the reader to adopt his sensible philosophy and put it to use. Or, an author can be so satiric and argumentative in tone that he could lead the reader to angry protest. The various tones and types of attitude that authors employ would make up quite an imposing list if one were to try. For example, here are some of the most popular and easily identified tones: cynical, impersonal, personal, rhetorical, serious, funny, ironical, irreverent, foolish, charming, teasing, sympathetic, frank, and humorous.

The following is a short paragraph from Charles Dickens's novel *Bleak House* [1] to demonstrate the hostile, slashing tone he uses in order to convey to his readers his strong dislike for the inefficiency of the English courts:

> Never can there come fog too thick, never can there come mud and mire too deep, to assort with the groping and floundering condition which this High Court of Chancery, most pestilent of hoary sinners, holds, this day, in the sight of heaven and earth.

Another passage that follows from Mrs. Gaskell's *Mary Barton* [2] holds an entirely different tone. It asks the reader to share in the pathos and sadness of the situation that the author implies in her own sympathetic tone and attitude toward death:

> She bent down and fondly, oh! with what passionate fondness, kissed her child, and then gave him up to Alice, who took him with tender care. Nature's struggles were soon exhausted, and he breathed his little life away in peace. Then the mother lifted up her voice and wept. Her cries brought her husband down to try with his aching heart to comfort hers. . .

And yet, an example of a third passage that has a contrasting tone to the above two in its frank and critical attitude towards its subject:

> Had there been proper motivation, nearly all of these young people could have found ways and means to obtain a professional education, and we would not be faced today with a deficiency of trained manpower. [3]

In conclusion, the management of tone has everything to do with the meaning the writer wishes to convey, and no matter what type of writing, the problem of tone is of utmost importance.

VII.   Grasping the Moral or Philosophical Attitude

Being asked to identify a philosophical or moral attitude in a literary work may sound at first like an overwhelmingly difficult task. But when

---

[1] Charles Dickens, *Bleak House* (London: Chapman & Hall, Ltd., 1906), p. 2.
[2] Elizabeth Gaskell, *Mary Barton*, 1 (London: Chapman & Hall, Ltd., 1848), p. 116.
[3] H. G. Rickover, "Let's Stop Wasting Our Greatest Resource," *The Saturday Evening Post* (March 2, 1957).

we strip the high-sounding words *philosophical* and *moral* of their abstractness, we find that the question could be put more plainly. In common terms we are asking: What does the author believe in? What basic stand does he take on this issue? What is his feeling toward life? Toward man? Toward beauty?

All *philosophy* deals essentially with the questions of: What is real? What is true? What is good? We are all philosophers in one way or another as we all tend to deal with the thoughts, principles, and facts of reality, and of human nature, and of human conduct.

Morality, often used synonymously with philosophy, is really a branch of philosophy or is to philosophy as a part is to a whole. Morality can be defined as specifically pertaining to standards of conduct and value. To hold a moral attitude is to have an opinion based on principles of right and wrong. To be a morally good person is to be virtuous, ethical, righteous, and noble. Of course, what can be morally right for one person may be morally wrong for another.

By defining philosophy and morality it can be seen that they are basic, and fundamental to the study of literature. For, it has often been said that literature helps us to lead a better life. We read and study in order to gain wisdom. The more we read, the more we are able to gain an insight into the complexity of human nature and into human motivation. Literature enables us to live life more fully than what our own direct experience allows. Through books we can develop an understanding of other people, other values, and other lands. Literature, as a humanistic study, is naturally concerned with the external questions of: What is life? What is good? What do men live by and for? We may have our own ideas or answers to these questions, but the more we read, the more we find that not everyone agrees with our concepts and not everyone reacts to the experiences of life as we do or as our own family does. Thus, to pick up an article or a book and merely read it without considering or penetrating the author's purpose for writing it is to miss the whole significance of his work.

True, there is some literature that has no deeper purpose than enjoyment or escape to a never-never land. Much material is written without any philosophical or moral intent. But, it would be terribly dull to restrict our channel of reading only to a Peter-Pan world of entertainment. Perhaps one of the most exciting and challenging reading activities instead is to be able to pick up an article, chapter, or whole book and express the writer's moral or philosophical attitude after reading it. Keep in mind what the author has to say—Does he agree with your concepts? Does he shed any light on a problem? Does he offer any solution to or interesting theory about his subject? Does he help you see that your view could be wrong, narrow, or inadequate? Or does the author increase your knowledge or introduce totally new thoughts?

In summary, to be able to express the moral or philosophical attitude is to pay careful attention to the points the author is trying to get across. Question yourself and see what view he has toward life or toward a certain experience. Oftimes the moral or philosophy behind the story or text is not obvious. It then becomes necessary to make deductions and inferences as to what the author means by the words, tone, and plot of the material.

VIII.   Making Correct Inferences

An *inference* is a logical conclusion drawn from given data or premises. Do not confuse inference with the word *assumption*, which means that something is taken for granted without proof.

From the above statements, it is clear that an inference must be based upon something which the author has said; that is, you must be able to place your finger on the lines as your proof. Of course, though you point your finger to certain lines, your inference is still "your interpretation" of those lines, and consequently subject to error.

The distinction that I am trying to make is this: you do not "dream up" an answer and simply say, "Well, that's the way I feel about it." No, an inference must be based on something said by the author. This means that when you are looking for an inference in a passage, you must look at the actual words and phrases of the material to determine the author's meaning, his reasoning, his logic, his purpose for the particular use of certain words.

In any passage under consideration, you must seek to find the author's attitude or feeling about a particular character, a group of characters, relationships among certain characters, type of society, forces of nature, events, religions, and so forth.

To illustrate how inferences are drawn, let us take a few examples of inference in literature. As the first example, consider James Thurber's short story, "The Secret Life of Walter Mitty." The story, as you know, concerns a day in the life of Walter Mitty. He and his wife are on a shopping trip in town. Mitty daydreams a great deal, and these daydreams are both stimulated and interrupted by his real life. Mitty's wife nags him often for his inattention to whatever he is doing. This, therefore, is the first judgment, the given datum or premise. From this we can then infer two possible situations: (1) Mitty's daydreaming is caused by his wife's nagging and his wish to escape, or (2) his wife's nagging is caused by Mitty's inattention. This is never really explained through the story itself. Therefore, since the author's attitude is not stated explicitly, we must seek elsewhere for information. Once we read his other writings and see his cartoons, we notice the repetition of the theme of the dominant female—dominant to the point of being overbearing. From this we can infer that Walter Mitty's daydreaming is caused by his wife's nagging. First we have the facts, which we then use to come to a conclusion.

Let's use another example. Karel Čapek said, "Man is something that feels happy, plays the piano, likes going for a walk, and in fact, wants to do a whole lot of things that are really unnecessary." The lines seem to say that man does many things that are useless. Some might interpret these lines in a moral sense: with so much poverty and need in this world, anyone who indulges himself beyond his needs is sinful. Yet from this quotation we can also infer the following: Man is something which does these things that appear to be unnecessary but actually are the fiber of a life of grace and civilization, as opposed to existence on the subsistence level. In such a case it is essential that we determine the author's purpose in writing the selection.

The third example is in the area of poetry. Poetry, of course, is inferential. The last two lines of Sandburg's poem "Grass" are a case in point: "I am the grass. Let me work." Upon first judgment, the data seem to be a simple statement, "I am the grass," and a simple request, "Let me work." Yet, from this poem one can see the implied antiwar bias. We infer that a battle is fiery and seemingly world-shaking at the time of its occurrence, but its traces are soon covered by time, and time is symbolized as grass—covering all.

These examples clearly show that the process of inferring is not something done in isolation; rather, the total skills of reading must be brought to bear upon the making of a decision—the inference.

IX. Recognizing the Functions of Descriptive Elements

Descriptive elements in writing may be used to point out the quality or condition of a scene, emotion, person, or event. It is this added quality or condition that gives richer meaning to a belief, point of view, or implication. Descriptive elements may be figures of speech, phrases, one word, or series of words. Descriptive elements may have any of the following purposes:

1. To establish the tone: personal-impersonal, satirical, ironical, humorous, cynical, amoral, emotive, moralistic, logical, figurative, rhetorical, philosophical.

2. To create an atmosphere: pastoral, romantic, weird, fantastic, of horror, of suspense, of peace, of violence, of frustration, of success.

3. To set up contrasts: to contrast one atmosphere with another, or one character with another.

4. To set up situation for commentary: to set the stages for presenting the author's point of view.

5. To develop characters: to set the stage for describing actions which give the reader a picture of the people about whom the author is writing.

6. To develop a scene or setting: to describe a scene out-of-doors, as well as indoors.

The following examples illustrate how descriptive elements are used to reveal much about a character who does the talking. We get an insight into the kind of person who is telling the story. The following excerpt is taken from "The Death of Red Peril," by Walter Edmonds: "And he lays down the dangest lump of worm you ever set your eyes on. It's the kind of insect a man might expect to see in a furrin' land." This bit of description not only tells you something about the worm, but much about the education and background of the person telling the story.

The second example shows how descriptive elements are used for presenting a picture. Robert Frost's poem, "Birches," provides a fine example. "You may see their trunks arching in the woods/ Years afterward, trailing their leaves on the ground."

In good writing descriptive elements are used with great precision, careful logic, and insight on the part of the author. The reader must give close attention to each word in a figure of speech, phrase, or series of adjectives. Descriptive elements give the author his particular qualities of style.

X. Determining the Author's Intent

Mickey Mantle, one of baseball's greats, has written a book about famous heroes of the sports' world. There are many inspiring stories of the struggles, sufferings, and personal problems that these athletes had to endure and overcome. But you will gain much more than pleasure and information from the book if you ask yourself at the outset, "Why did Mantle write these stories? What did he try to accomplish?" This sense of anticipation can lead you to see his intent: to inspire young people to follow the examples of determination and courage which these great athletes had displayed in daily life.

How do you find the author's intention in a passage or book? Anticipation is important, but needs to be supplemented by more concrete information.

In seeking to find the author's intent, you are not trying to find one specific statement which summarizes his whole purpose in writing; if you can find one, the author is not a very imaginative writer. As you read, consider which of the following three types of results is being sought by the author.

1. Is his main purpose to give information so that you will have more accurate *knowledge* of his subject?
2. Does he intend to give you a certain *feeling* about a person or problem presented in the book? Is it, then, that he is concerned mainly with your *attitude*?
3. Is it his main intent to provoke specific *action* as a result of your reading his work. Does he mainly want you to *do* something?

Of course, all three elements may be present to some extent, but deciding which is prominent will help guide you in finding the exact content that is related to the knowledge, feeling, or action the author is seeking to promote. In the example of Mantle's book, you will discover he is mainly concerned with feeling and attitude, rather than knowledge or particular action.

Suppose we try to tie in three elements which have already been explained to help you grasp the "content" of the author's intention. First, the pattern of development may give an important clue about his intent, so you should always be asking, "How is he developing the story? What elements are crucial in it?"

Second, try to sense the tone of the passage or book, especially if there is a sudden shift of tone. The author's intent will be clearer if you are alert for this.

Third, what is his moral or philosophical viewpoint? In all serious writing, discovering this is invaluable in unfolding his intention. These three elements, then, should be in the back of your mind throughout the entire reading process.

DATE DUE

MAR 3 0 1982			

GAYLORD | | | PRINTED IN U.S.A.